How to Have Difficult Conversations as an Educational Leader

This valuable new book helps school and district leaders build trust and credibility through meaningful conversations, even in the messiest situations. Starting with a good look at self-awareness, this book walks you through strategies to prepare for and have effective conversations with employees and colleagues. Rich in reflective exercises and real-life examples, you'll finish this book with a better understanding of your own purpose, confidence, and wellness, and why all this matters to being a successful communicator. You will also have at your fingertips the specific steps to prepare for difficult meetings, start meetings with a clear outcome, listen with purpose and intent, implement a discussion effectively in any situation, and successfully close the meeting. This engaging book covers some of the most difficult scenarios confronted by principals, assistant principals, directors, and school district leaders, including performance feedback, meetings involving investigations, misconduct, disagreement, and delivering hard messages. Difficult conversations and holding other adults accountable can be overwhelming and intimidating, but armed with this book, you'll know how to effectively provide feedback to further build trusting relationships with your school staff.

Patty Corum, Ed.D., is an educational trainer and speaker, and has 28 years' previous experience in public education as a teacher, principal, and deputy superintendent.

Also Available from Routledge Eye on Education
(www.routledge.com/eyeoneducation)

Making Community Schools a Reality: Harnessing Your Power as a School Leader through Collaboration
Emily L. Woods

Wholehearted School Leadership: Rewiring Our Schools for Courage, Justice, Learning, and Connection
Kathryn Fishman-Weaver

Data Analysis for Continuous School Improvement
Victoria L. Bernhardt

Teacher Leadership Practice in High-Performing Schools: A Blueprint for Excellence
Jeremy D. Visone

Culturally Conscious Decision-Making for School Leaders: A Toolkit for Creating a More Equitable School Culture
Shauna McGee

Coaching Education Leaders: A Culturally Responsive Approach to Transforming Schools and Systems
Nancy B. Gutiérrez, Michelle Jarney, and Michael Kim

Fostering Parent Engagement for Equitable and Successful Schools: A Leader's Guide to Supporting Families and Students
Patrick Darfler-Sweeney

Finding Your Path as a Woman in School Leadership: A Guide for Educators, Allies, and Advocates
Kim Cofino and Christina Botbyl

A Leadership Playbook for Addressing Rapid Change in Education: Empowered for Success
Teresa L. San Martín

Improving Teacher Morale and Motivation: Leadership Strategies That Build Student Success
Ronald Williamson and Barbara R. Blackburn

Lead with Truth: How to Make a Difference in Your School, Your Life, and the Lives of Your Students
Qiana O'Leary

When Black Students Excel: How Schools Can Engage and Empower Black Students
Joseph F. Johnson, Jr., Cynthia L. Uline, and Stanley J. Munro, Jr.

How to Have Difficult Conversations as an Educational Leader

Self-Reflections and Strategies for Success

Patty Corum

Routledge
Taylor & Francis Group
NEW YORK AND LONDON

First published 2026
by Routledge
605 Third Avenue, New York, NY 10158

and by Routledge
4 Park Square, Milton Park, Abingdon, Oxon, OX14 4RN

Routledge is an imprint of the Taylor & Francis Group, an informa business

© 2026 Patty Corum

The right of Patty Corum to be identified as author of this work has been asserted in accordance with sections 77 and 78 of the Copyright, Designs and Patents Act 1988.

All rights reserved. No part of this book may be reprinted or reproduced or utilised in any form or by any electronic, mechanical, or other means, now known or hereafter invented, including photocopying and recording, or in any information storage or retrieval system, without permission in writing from the publishers.

Trademark notice: Product or corporate names may be trademarks or registered trademarks, and are used only for identification and explanation without intent to infringe.

Library of Congress Cataloging-in-Publication Data
Names: Corum, Patty, author.
Title: How to have difficult conversations as an educational leader: self-reflections and strategies for success / Patty Corum.
Description: New York, NY: Routledge, 2026. |
Includes bibliographical references. |
Identifiers: LCCN 2025017644 (print) | LCCN 2025017645 (ebook) | ISBN 9781041071167 (hardback) | ISBN 9781041071150 (paperback) | ISBN 9781003638902 (ebook)
Subjects: LCSH: Educational leadership. | Communication in education.
Classification: LCC LB2805 .C6594 2026 (print) | LCC LB2805 (ebook) | DDC 371.2/011—dc23/eng/20250617
LC record available at https://lccn.loc.gov/2025017644
LC ebook record available at https://lccn.loc.gov/2025017645

ISBN: 978-1-041-07116-7 (hbk)
ISBN: 978-1-041-07115-0 (pbk)
ISBN: 978-1-003-63890-2 (ebk)

DOI: 10.4324/9781003638902

Typeset in Warnock Pro
by codeMantra

Contents

Meet the Author — ix
Acknowledgments — xi
Preface — xv
Why Read *How to Have Difficult Conversations as an Educational Leader?* — xv
Let It Be the Journey That It Is! — xvi
One Step at a Time — xvii
Scenarios and Lessons Learned — xx

▶ Step 1: Self-Reflections — 1

Introduction — 1
Know Your Purpose — 2
Name Your Past — 4
Understand How Others View You and Why It Matters — 7
Take Care of You — 11
Embrace Your Control and Let Go of the Rest — 22
Summary — 39
Reflection Exercises — 39
Bibliography — 43

▶ Step 2: Prepare for the Conversation — 45

The Importance of Planning — 45
Know Policies and Precedent — 46
Understand the Person — 49
Know Their Patterns — 51
Articulate the Problem — 52
Name the Purpose for the Conversation — 54
Plan for Follow-Up — 55
Summary — 56
Reflection Exercises — 57

▶ Step 3: Learn to Listen — 59

The Gift of Listening	59
Plan for Listening	62
Make Listening a Habit	64
Listening in Difficult Situations	65
Reflection Exercises	72
Bibliography	73

▶ Step 4: Meet with Success — 75

It Is Time to Meet	75
Name the Outcome	75
Ask Good Questions	79
Use Care and Clarity	80
Consider Your Delivery	84
Facilitate Closure	103
Reflection Exercises	105
Bibliography	107

▶ Step 5: Conversation Follow Up — 109

Why Follow Up?	109
Follow Up to Touch Base	110
Follow Up to Show Support	112
Follow Up to Provide Feedback	115
Follow Up Because You Expect Action	117
Follow Up with Documentation	120
Follow Up to Correct Something You Did	127
Remember the Humans	130
Reflection Exercises	134
Bibliography	135

Final Remarks	137
Closing Thoughts	137
Consider Your Next Difficult Conversation	138
My Hope for You	140

Meet the Author

I am an educational trainer and speaker who works with school administrators in various areas of leadership and effective communication and have worked with numerous school districts and universities in Missouri and South Carolina. My speaking engagements and training sessions include learning and practicing how to have difficult conversations effectively, how to provide meaningful performance feedback and coaching to faculty and staff, and how to develop a strong self-awareness so we can better communicate and connect as we lead.

Along with my training and speaking engagements, I served as the Executive Director of the Missouri Association of School Personnel Administrators (MOASPA) for ten years, and for over two decades, worked with the Missouri Department of Elementary and Secondary Education (DESE) in various projects related to leadership development. I have been an instructor and guest instructor in educational leadership programs at St. Louis University, University of Missouri – St. Louis, University of Missouri – Columbia, and Lindenwood University.

Prior to my current work, I spent 28 years in public education as a teacher, principal, assistant superintendent for human resources, and finally deputy superintendent, where I retired in 2014 from Fort Zumwalt, a large school district outside of St. Louis, Missouri. I earned a Bachelor's Degree in Elementary Education, Master's Degree and Educational Specialist Degree in Educational Administration, and Educational Doctorate in Educational Leadership and Policy Analysis from the University of Missouri, Columbia.

It was from these experiences as a graduate student, teacher, and leader, I learned that communication can be difficult even when it seems like it should be easy. I found myself in situations where messages were hard, relationships troubled, or perspectives different, and I found in those circumstances, connecting was even more challenging. I spent years watching great leaders excel, while weak ones lose respect, status, and influence due to their lack of ability to have a difficult conversation effectively.

Subsequently, I began to put together lists of strategies, dispositions, and language that seemed to be working for others. I also practiced myself, and it became clear to me. There are, in fact, certain things that can be done to increase the likelihood for meaningful conversations even in difficult situations. Ultimately, it resulted in more productive problem-solving, more positive school environments, better relationships, and daily peace in my life.

I continue to enjoy the benefits of effective communication, and most notably, I am more comfortable with myself, listening, understanding, reflecting, and accepting. I am happier in the spaces I find myself, and my mind has stopped racing at night. I no longer dread upcoming difficult conversations or uncomfortable situations. Instead, by building a stronger me, and practicing steps to approach, implement, and follow up on difficult conversations, I have become better equipped for life and leadership.

And so, being a part of educational leadership is a tremendous gift. The work is challenging and complex, and can even be gut-wrenching, yet at the same time, I have found it to be fulfilling, interesting, fun, and worthwhile. My ability to persevere in hard times and be satisfied along the way is because of so many great leaders and people in my life who taught me valuable lessons I will never forget. It is now my responsibility and pleasure to pass my learning along to you.

When I am not writing, training, and engaging with educational leaders, my greatest loves are spending time with family and friends, traveling, and enjoying long walks on the beach. It is within these moments alone, and moments spent with the people I love the most, that I find opportunity to immerse myself in gratitude and solace, and remember the many fortunes in my life.

Acknowledgments

I want to thank my family, starting with the most supportive and encouraging mom and dad anyone could ever have, John (1932–2004) and Alberta (1936–2024) Corum. They believed in me every step, and were so proud in 1986 when I became a sixth-grade teacher in Hallsville, Missouri. I will never forget the many conversations around their kitchen table, or sitting on the patio next to the garden, discussing life, education, leadership, and children. They were my first teachers, and not a day goes by when I do not think of both, how they might handle a situation, or what they taught me to prepare for life. I am also grateful for all the Corums in my life, my sister, Pam (1958–2014), and my brothers and their wives, Bryan and Jane Corum, Bob and Jeanice Corum, and all my nieces and nephews. As the youngest of four children, I owe much to my family for helping make me strong, instilling important values, and knowing that family, laughter, love, and sticking together are important cornerstones in life.

In 1996, I married Dr. Brent Underwood. Brent is a retired school superintendent and former teacher, assistant principal, principal, and area superintendent. We met at an elementary principal conference, and we have been "talking school" ever since. Brent has always encouraged me to follow my dreams, whether that means being a keynote speaker to a room full of hundreds of educators, or sitting on the beach with a friend or a grandchild, waiting for the next sunset. He is often by my side in my endeavors and is a genuinely supportive colleague, friend, and husband.

I am very fortunate to have three stepchildren and their spouses in my life, Ryan Underwood and his wife Trish, Matthew Underwood and his wife Alicia, and Casey Underwood and her husband, Nick Hanger, and I cannot imagine life without them! They have taught me more in the last 30 years than I can ever write in one book and I love them enormously! Their mom, Karen Underwood, is a strong, loving, and generous mom, grandma, and friend, and has inspired me over the years with her strength and kindness. We have four beautiful grandchildren, Macklin, Miles, Riley, and Tate, who simply make our world a better place!

I must also thank the hundreds of influential educational leaders in my life with whom I have shared this awesome journey. They are the true inspiration for this book, and without their influence and friendship, I would not be the person or the leader I am today. The ideas contained within these chapters, and the many lessons learned, come from the interactions and relationships with these important colleagues!

Finally, I would like to thank six people who were carefully selected and agreed to provide input on my book prior to its submission to the publisher. While they are at different points in their journeys and hold distinctive positions in work and life, they have all been important encouragers of my efforts.

Jacob Clark. I have known Jacob and his family since he was in early elementary school. Jacob, a high school math teacher and coach, comes from a loving family. He is now following in the footsteps of his accomplished and talented father, Dr. Jon Clark, a former math teacher and high school principal. Jacob has an amazing personal presence and demonstrates leadership qualities like being a great listener, an astute learner, and an amazing teacher. For someone who is in the beginning of his career, he already demonstrates profound abilities in connecting with others through compassion and hard work.

Dr. Kristin Denbow. Kristin has been a close friend for many years. We have done many of the same things, teacher, principal, assistant superintendent, and university instructor in educational leadership, and I am honored to get to work with her and receive her professional collaboration and friendship. She is smart and kind, and has a wealth of information. I continue to value her insight and expertise.

Meg Holliday. Meg, an assistant principal in a district where I conduct training, is a spirited, smart, grateful, and positive participant and leader. She is eager to learn from others and has much to offer as a school administrator. I have been inspired by her insight and talent in connecting with others.

Joe Sutton. I met Joe in about 2000 when I became assistant superintendent in the Fort Zumwalt School District. After serving as a teacher and assistant principal, Joe was the Principal at

Fort Zumwalt North High School for many years. Upon meeting and working with him, I found Joe to be the kind of leader I wanted to emulate – kind, attentive, smart, respectful, hard-working, and reliable. He is an expert leader and a kind human being.

Ilene Osherow. I became friends with Ilene when we moved into our current home in 2012. She lived close by, and upon getting to know her, I learned that I not only had a new neighbor but also a new friend. Ilene was a real estate agent during her working years and continues to enjoy a full life as a mom, grandma, great-grandma, and friend to many. She has influenced me over the years because of her unique ability to love unconditionally, listen with curiosity and care, build meaningful relationships, and live life to its very fullest.

Barbara Underwood. Barbara is my mother-in-law and friend. She was a teacher at Parkway West High School for nearly 30 years and was Missouri's Teacher of the Year in 1976. Barbara led the Parkway Education Association for teachers during her years as a teacher leader and understands lots about leadership in schools. I continue to appreciate our time together and meaningful conversations.

Dr. Brent Underwood. Already mentioned, but should be mentioned again, this time as a reader. Brent, my husband, and constant collaborator spent hours reading, listening to, and discussing every single aspect of this work. His partnership, honesty, and guidance are everywhere in my thinking and in my writing.

Preface

▶ WHY READ *HOW TO HAVE DIFFICULT CONVERSATIONS AS AN EDUCATIONAL LEADER?*

The most striking revelation upon entering school leadership for many new administrators is the realization that communication with adults can be complicated and even frightening. Many educational leaders spend years in the classroom teaching children and as such, develop a sense of savvy when it comes to communicating with 5-year-olds and 16-year-olds, and we feel pretty good about it. Then comes administration. Upon entry, we are now dealing with people who might be twice our age, years more experienced, and significantly more knowledgeable. Over the course of their lifetime, adults have had years to acquire assumptions, intellectual capacity, bias, personality traits, skepticism, and communication habits which can make our interactions with them more convoluted. Working with adults is different from working with children. The dynamics can vary greatly. The consequences can be staggering. As an educational leader, how do we approach another adult and value them, while also holding them accountable for work in the school? It starts with positive connections and the ability to have productive conversations, even in difficult situations.

    I have written this book to help school leaders build trust and credibility through meaningful conversations, even in messy situations. It focuses on adult connections that administrators must have to effectively lead in a school environment. Starting with a good look at ourselves, we walk through steps and strategies to prepare for, have, and follow up on difficult conversations with the adults in our schools. My hope is that you will gain a better understanding of your own purpose, tendencies, confidence, image, control, and wellness and why it matters. You will consider specific steps to prepare for hard meetings, listen with purpose and intent, start meetings with a clear outcome, implement a discussion effectively no matter what, and successfully close the meeting and follow up.

Throughout this book, I present numerous real-life educational scenarios that demonstrate how effective administrators successfully prepare for, connect, communicate, and follow up with school employees using certain attitudes, specific techniques, and intentional steps. Suggestions presented have been used over and over by successful school leaders, including my colleagues and mentors, as well as myself, for over 40 years.

For most successful leaders and practitioners, learning and growing is a journey that never ends. By contemplating your communication and connection with others on a regular basis, while attending to your own communication style, strengths, goals, control, and wellness, conversations can be more productive and stress-free, relationships more affirming, and life more peaceful. Overall, these are the most prominent lessons I learned as an educational leader.

▶ LET IT BE THE JOURNEY THAT IT IS!

Effective communication is a journey, and improvement and excellence take time. That is the good news! We are always preparing for the next thing life brings. You are more prepared to purchase your next home, after you have bought and sold a few houses. Once you have ridden the subway in New York, or flown a certain airline a few times, you are more prepared for the next trip. While each event is different, the mere familiarity prepares you for what might happen the next time. The same can be said for communication. If you have never spoken in public, that first time can be scary. But once you have done it a few times, and have acquired some know-how, some understanding about what to expect and how it feels, it becomes easier to navigate. Now consider a difficult conversation with an employee or a colleague. Those are uncomfortable at best, but when you have practiced, and had some success in the past, you begin to cultivate the necessary approaches, attitudes, and behaviors to make subsequent conversations go more smoothly.

> Isn't that a refreshing thought? Each encounter gives us something to learn and something to consider about how we might handle a similar situation in the future.

What a gift! It means that this difficult experience is not going to be the last. It means it does not have to be perfect. You will realize that with each conversation, some strategies work better than others. When you find success, you will likely repeat that behavior. Now, add to that your growing self-awareness and ability to present in a clear, calm, and understanding way. Add your growing ability to listen without judgment, realize what you can control, stop trying to control what you cannot, know when to talk and when to let silence happen, and so on. Your journey includes learning about yourself as well as learning about the techniques that make communication better and messy situations more productive.

This way of thinking allows us to make mistakes. It gives us permission to slow down, ponder, and absorb. It reminds us that each daily interaction is not the end, but rather it is a journey and our goal is to do better each time, to connect more successfully, be more prepared, listen better, and engage more fully. As you gain experiences and continue to more fully understand the nuance of human dynamics, especially in messy situations and school leadership, you will get better. My hope is that as you read, you will discover all the above as you make your way through your leadership journey. Breathe, enjoy, learn, be vulnerable, and be yourself.

▶ ONE STEP AT A TIME

Yes, it is a journey, and the journey is more doable when you think about it in terms of steps. It will not all come together at the same time on the same day; however, if you know yourself and your tendencies, stack your strategies, build your strengths, continue to reflect, and take one step at a time, you will continue to feel more confident about your communication, even when the messages and the meetings are hard. *How to Have Difficult Conversations as an Educational Leader* is presented in steps for easier digestion, thoughtful consideration, and practical action.

I have learned that the first step in just about anything we do is being a strong you. It is tough to embark on difficult things, like school administration and hard conversations with other adults, if you are not stable, grounded, regulated, and confident. Step 1, Self-Reflections, asks the reader to consider several aspects of self-awareness as a school leader. We start with consideration to who we are, why we are, and what we are doing here, in this space, in this job, and with these responsibilities.

I suggest you reflect on your purpose and mission daily as you make your way through educational leadership and life. It will help uphold (or contradict) your decisions, remind you of why you do the activities you do every day, and keep you focused on where you are going. In addition to knowing your why, ponder where you come from, who grew you, and why you have the strengths, beliefs, and tendencies you have today. Who influenced you to be the way you are and why is that important as you live life? Another aspect of knowing yourself better so that you can be more "other-centered" as an educational leader is to think about your external self-awareness and how others view you. Consider your image and why that matters in leadership. How others view you has huge impact on your ability to lead them successfully.

Furthermore, wellness, how we take care of ourselves physically, emotionally, spiritually, intellectually, socially, and occupationally, is another piece of self-awareness that builds confidence and strength in school administrators. This section takes you through six domains of self-care and provides reflection about how you are attending to your own needs so you can be stronger for others.

Finally, and importantly, a big component of my soul-searching journey is the concept of control, remembering every day, and with every situation, what I control, what I do not control, and how I use my power to dictate my thoughts, attitudes, dispositions, actions, reactions, and interactions with others. If I spend time perseverating on the things over which I have no control, it will paralyze my actions and ability to successfully lead. Read and reflect on how you think about your control over your own life and daily activities, thoughts, and attitudes.

Once we have reflected on our own identity and know ourselves, we can move on to preparing for those difficult conversations. While the concept of self-awareness and self-care should never be far from your thinking, Step 2, Prepare for the Conversation, takes us further down the road into thinking about our conversations, our relationships, and the issues with which we must address as school leaders. You would never have a big dinner party, go on vacation with your children, or make a huge investment without some planning. Why then, do we sometimes enter difficult conversations without specific preparation? When difficult conversations are imminent, we tend to focus on our own worry and self-doubt, perhaps missing the opportunity to sit down and properly plan. In this step, consider knowing your context (policies and precedent), understanding the person with whom you are meeting, having observed their patterns, being able to articulate the alleged problem or issue, and stating the purpose of the meeting. When you are well prepared, the conversation is much more likely to have a positive outcome.

Step 3, Learn to Listen, provides suggestions and examples that consider meaningful and thorough listening, a cornerstone to good communication and a gift to the people around you. Listening to understand, not to respond will help build better connections, trust, and credibility, not to mention, it will help you move forward in a more meaningful and productive way. Listening makes people want to come back and share more. Listening demonstrates a sense of other-centeredness and compassion. Listening shows people you value them. Listening makes you smarter and more prepared to move forward. Listening exhibits maturity and the ability to be still and focused.

Moving on, the next step, after taking a good look at yourself, thorough preparation, and constantly learning to be a better listener, it is time to have the meeting. In Step 4, Meet with Success, leaders will consider everything from the format of the discussion (stating the outcome, asking good questions, listening, staying on track, and a good closure) to strategies and considerations we can use to facilitate a productive meeting. In this section, learn to chunk the conversation into different components with a clear outcome in mind. Consider your approach to stating hard messages as well as productive responses when the other person reacts in certain ways.

Finally, Step 5, Conversation Follow-Up, includes many reasons and ways to follow up with professionals after a difficult conversation. Nothing happens in complete isolation; rather, building a relationship, solving a problem, or contributing to the never-ending evolution of school culture happens through a series of interactions. Making sure that we follow up with people, when action is needed, and even when it is not, is critical in leadership. Read more scenarios, and consider the power and influence of follow-up in this final step.

Throughout *How to Have Difficult Conversations as an Educational Leader*, you will have the opportunity to participate in some reflection exercises at the end of each section. These are meant to help you be in constant contemplation about yourself, your attitudes, your approaches, your strategies, and your success. As you consider each step, examine how one relates to and impacts another. Combine aspects of your disposition and tactics, for enhanced impact. Celebrate the milestones as you begin to master areas of communication and having difficult conversations. Pay attention to your journey. What you do and how you do it impacts your success.

SCENARIOS AND LESSONS LEARNED

This section is presented as a reference to various educational scenarios presented in *How to Have Difficult Conversations as an Educational Leader*. If you find yourself wanting to remember a scenario, but cannot remember the section, you can refer to this list to find the situation, the step where it lives in this book, and the lessons learned.

TOM THE ANGRY TECH, a tech who gets angry during phone calls, even cussing and yelling, which results in my colleague having lots of anxiety and stress.. Found in Step 1. Remember what you control, and let go of the rest. State your boundaries, and when the difficult conversation is over, do not allow the other person to take up space in your head.

ELLEN THE EXCUSE MAKER, an experienced early childhood teacher whose classroom is overcrowded with materials, limiting space for children. Found in Step 1. Execute the control you have in setting the pace, the tone, and the direction of a difficult meeting. You have the power to keep the meeting on track.

STEVE THE STORYTELLER, an effective teacher with some great strategies, however often gets longwinded in his own stories, leaving students bored and unengaged. Found in Step 3. Ask good questions and then listen to understand. Sometimes, the other person will solve the problem themselves.

CONFIDENT CAROL, a new teacher who is overly confident in her teaching and relationships, and has some behaviors that need to be corrected. Found in Step 3. Listen with curiosity, not judgment. Then, listen more. The more you understand the person and the situation, the better prepared you are to facilitate meaningful support.

MARK THE MILD-MANNERED SPECIAL EDUCATION TEACHER, a first-year teacher who is called to meet with the Director of Special Education for an unknown reason. Found in Step 4. Tell the person the purpose of the meeting. The participant will be more at ease, and the meeting will go more smoothly.

ERICA THE EMPATHETIC COORDINATOR, a curriculum coordinator and teacher leader who seems to be opposing administration about a tough new curriculum. Found in Step 4. Be very clear about what you hope to accomplish in the meeting. This helps you stay on track and accomplish something specific.

NATE THE NICE GUY, a tech who is kind to others in his work, but doesn't realize it. Found in Step 4. We show compassion in different ways. While there is no right or wrong way, try to include care in your conversations.

MATT THE MAINTENANCE MAN, an employee who continues to neglect completion tags as required, even after being asked. Found in Step 4. Silence is Golden. Silence allows time for the other person to think and to share. Do not do the talking for them.

TALIA THE TEXTER, a teacher who is violating district technology policy by texting students individually. Found in Step 4. Silence is Golden. When you are seeking information, you must be quiet and give the other person time to consider what they are willing to share. The more time you give, the more likely they are to share.

UMA THE UNION PRESIDENT, a teacher who reports that mold in a certain wing of the school is causing people to get sick. Found in Step 4. Do Not Talk about What You Do Not Know About. Instead, ask good questions and let the person know you need to do some checking and will get back to them.

TARA THE TEACHER OF THE YEAR, an experienced and well-regarded teacher leader who has a classroom observation that leaves the administrator with questions about her effectiveness. Found in Step 4. Consider Technology or No Technology. There can be some negative consequences if you do something electronically that should have been done in person.

STEVE THE STORYTELLER, an effective teacher with some great strategies, however often gets longwinded in his own stories, leaving students bored and unengaged. Part II found in Step 4. Facilitate closure so the meeting participant and you are on the same page about what happened in the meeting and what is next.

TIMESHEET TYLER, a custodian who is having medical concerns and is leaving early and not reporting time accurately. Found in Step 5. Following up with people is a critical next step after a difficult meeting. One of the best ways to show support is by getting back to them on the issue.

STEVE THE STORYTELLER, an effective teacher with some great strategies, however often gets longwinded in his own stories, leaving students bored and unengaged. Part III found in Step 5. Sometimes following up means giving specific feedback on how the person is implementing the suggestions given. This can be a powerful show of leadership and development for your staff.

CONFIDENT CAROL, a new teacher who is overly confident in her teaching and relationships, and has some behaviors that need to be corrected. Part II found in Step 5. Follow-up can take the form of ensuring someone is complying with your request or directives. It often includes written documentation.

MICHAEL THE MISTAKE MAKER, a new high school math teacher who seems confused about his content while teaching. Found in Step 5. Documentation is critical when following up difficult situations with improvement plans.

TARA THE TEACHER OF THE YEAR, an experienced and well-regarded teacher leader who has a classroom observation that leaves the administrator with questions about her effectiveness. Part II found in Step 5. Sometimes you must just go back to the person, say you made a mistake, apologize, and move forward.

RACHEL THE REPORTER, a teacher leader who bypasses the school principal and reports seemingly minor problems to the superintendent. Found in Step 5. Remember, people are human beings. In messy situations, think about your angle and which part of the big picture you will focus on with the other person. Lean in on the aspect that has a better chance of building relationships and trust. Feel free to bypass the parts of the situation that promote blame or perpetuate grudges.

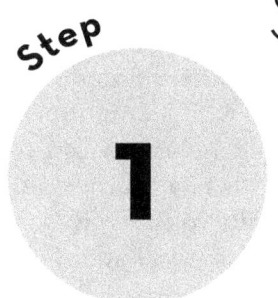

Self-Reflections

▶ INTRODUCTION

Whether it is a difficult conversation, a leadership dilemma, or complex decision-making, most experienced school administrators would agree, before we can adequately throw ourselves into effectively leading, it helps to be grounded and comfortable with ourselves. We should feel confident and strong. It helps to be able to think about other people and problems without being distracted by our own insecurities, needs, and judgments. We should be able to listen without becoming defensive. We should be able to focus without getting sidetracked by internal instincts or external noise. We ought to be able to act authentically without feeling controlled by others. A strong sense of self, and the ability to understand and manage our emotions, control, thoughts, words, and actions, will help us better connect with others. The better we connect, the more likely we are to engage and lead effectively, even when the situation at hand is difficult.

It is a little like needing that initial cup of coffee in the morning, before starting the first work task. For different people it is different things that stabilize us and get us ready for the day, but the idea is universal. We know the importance of being strong enough to handle life and people, and how ever we get there is up to us. In watching great educational leaders over four decades, I have discovered that this idea, working on YOU first, is key to successful, meaningful, purposeful, and productive leadership, including and especially facilitating difficult conversations.

> Being a strong you, may be the best learning you can do as you prepare for leadership

A sense of efficacy and belief in your own ability to execute, along with commitment to continued learning, and reflection can be essential. Knowing that this is a journey and not a destination will liberate you and give you permission to ponder your growth and make mistakes. We will never perform flawlessly but we can get better, be more humble, kinder, more logical, and clearer-minded as we go.

If you watch strong and successful leaders around you, notice their level of self-identity. This should not be confused with self-centeredness or arrogance. A strong self-awareness in part is simply the ability to know yourself at a level to which you can be still and focus on others. It is the confidence that demonstrates knowledge, maturity, humility, and integrity, no matter what age or how many years you have been in the profession. A strong self-awareness provides an understanding of our own strengths, weaknesses, biases, needs, triggers, control, and purpose. It means we know who we are, to the point to which we can selflessly understand and serve others. Wherever you are in your leadership journey, there are things you can do to advance your level of self-awareness and confidence.

▶ KNOW YOUR PURPOSE

Experts in leadership are constantly reminding us of the importance of naming our why or knowing our purpose. Many interview tools and leadership assessments in the education space spend time explaining the benefit of knowing why you chose education, even crafting a mission and vision, and being able to articulate your purpose to others. Educational experts and practitioners place tremendous value on organizations and individuals determining and displaying their purpose statements.

What tends to be true for most educators, in general, is that we enter the profession because we feel a higher calling, specifically an urge to help others. We are motivated, not by the paycheck or school calendar, but by the fact that we are educating children, supporting families, and contributing to the development of future communities. During thousands of interviews which I conducted for three decades as a school leader, one of the most important questions I asked was why the person wanted to be a teacher or principal. I listened for deliberate reasons about their desires to teach a child to read, support, and develop teachers, or work with others to provide a healthy school culture. I knew through experiences and through educational research that a strong purpose matters when it comes to success in education. Having a clear and meaningful commitment is one of the greatest factors that preamps teaching and leadership success. It is a critical variable when it comes to job performance, harmony, and longevity in the profession.

When it comes to having hard conversations, you are more likely to approach an employee when there is a problem, if you know your why. When you can state the correlation between your purpose for being a school administrator and your purpose for having a difficult conversation, you are more inclined to do it and to try to do it successfully. If, for example, your mission (your why) in school leadership is that "stronger adults grow stronger, more successful students," then you realize your actions should revolve around supporting and developing teachers and support staff. Having a strong sense of purpose gives you not only permission, but also motivation and urgency to reach out, communicate with, support, and hold accountable those who work with the learners within your community.

As a long-time educational leader, I continue to spend time each day considering my why. I ask myself these questions every morning before I get out of bed. Who am I? Why am I? What am I doing here? I believe in a higher power, and I trust that I am here for a reason. I know my strengths lie in education and leadership. I believe I am here to be generous and to help others. I value family and believe that the stronger we are as a unit, the better existence each person can enjoy. Knowing my why gives me direction as I ponder my goals for the day. In my daily meditation, I consider how my actions are a part of my why, and how everything I do adds meaning to the life I have chosen to live. As I talk with other successful leaders, they too find a great deal of importance in contemplating their purpose on a regular basis. It helps us stay on

> Naming your purpose gives value to your work and your life.

track, say no to the things that do not fit, continue to strengthen ourselves and our capacity and find meaning and happiness in what we do. It gives us motivation to fight a good fight, be silent when that is the better choice, and live and work with meaningful intention.

▶ NAME YOUR PAST

One way to increase self-awareness and build confidence is to spend time reflecting on who you are and why you are, with regard to your past. We are all greatly impacted by the people in our past and those who currently surround us. It seems impossible to spend time with people and not be impacted by them one way or another. We evolve with every impression of and interaction with others. We consider their beliefs, their actions, and their dispositions. We notice how they appear, behave, communicate, and interact. We make judgments about whether we are comfortable with them, and even if we want to imitate some of what we are observing. Think of the people who influence you in three categories:

Those who were with us in our formative years
Those who have influenced us as adults from a distance
Those who we credit for impacting us in the most powerful ways through close relationships.

Start with your formative years. This is where it seems we may have been the most deeply affected. Those who had the greatest hand in raising us and teaching us early on likely had more influence than we realize. Experiences from early childhood through adolescence probably shaped our beliefs, attitudes, self-esteem, emotional triggers, and tendencies when it comes to relationships and communication. They may have had a great influence on who we vote for, our faith, sense of right and wrong, or how we view and treat other people. Think about your beliefs, values, and propensities, and see what kinds of connections you can find to your early surroundings. To invest time in considering your past might prove helpful.

Now think about those people who helped shape you in your adulthood from a distance, as you were determining what you wanted life to look like for you. Who did you watch online, on stage, or in books, and consider their accomplishments, platforms, or presence? Who challenged you to think about your path or your career in certain ways? Who were your greatest role models or heroes who you did not know but who impacted your life? As a female born in the 1960s, I think of figures like Jackie Kennedy Onassis, Serena Williams, and Mary Tyler Moore to name a few. Over the years I read and watched women who, to me, represented strength, independence, confidence, and change. Some of the people I admired from afar showed me how to blaze a trail amid pushback and difficult conditions. They stayed focused, introduced new ideas, stood up for what was right, and worked long and hard to fulfill their own dreams.

In addition to famous people, I watched educational leaders whom I did not know, but admired. They included certain superintendents and principals from around my state who led with confidence, knowledge, clarity, and kindness. Although none of these people were involved in raising me in any way, they influenced my way of thinking about my future and how I envisioned myself as a leader. In some cases, it was women in the 1980s or 1990s who navigated their way through an educational landscape made up of mostly men. Sometimes it was the only African American leader in the room, whose singularity did not stop them from being a strong and engaged leader. It may do you well to think of those people for yourself, name their appealing characteristics, and as you do your daily reflection consider why they made such an impression on you. Continue to remember their impact on you as you further your educational journey.

Finally, consider the people who have had or are having the most direct impact on you personally and professionally. These are or have been significant players in your life. They are more than the virtual influencers, celebrities, athletes, actors, authors, or educational role models you have never met. These are people who have touched you in the most personal way, people who have or have had a relationship with you, and who know you and believe in you. These are the people who have your best interest in mind, people who coach you and mentor you in honest and caring ways. As you share with them and ask for help and advice, they are not in it for themselves, they are in it for you! These people might include mom, dad, other close relatives, spouses, teachers, coaches, best friends, or close professional colleagues. They might be people who are still alive or they might have passed, but they are people who continue to have a profound impact on how you live.

There are two reasons to consider the people throughout our lives who influenced us the most. The first is simply to be aware and to spend time thinking about role models from your past and present, who have impressed upon you significantly. It is enlightening to ponder the memories and relationships. It can be useful to rethink who they are and how you might want to emulate their behaviors and dispositions in your life and leadership. It is worth it to think, "How would Dr. Peach handle a situation like this," for example, or "What would my dad say about that?" You may do that regularly anyway, but a concerted effort will no doubt pay off. When you list five or ten or even twenty of these people whom you admire, who you believe played a critical role in your success and happiness, write it down. Display it for a while to implant not only those people, but also their traits, in your mind. It does not mean you are trying to be just like them; it simply means we all have role models and people we admire who have done great things, likely through kindness, hard work, integrity, intention, self-awareness, and a journey of constant learning and sharing.

> Bring those people into your consciousness. Remember why you admire them. Think about their influence as you encounter difficult situations. Perhaps, it is time to jot them a note and let them know the explicit and positive influence they had on you.

Another reason to spend time thinking about your people is to give yourself permission to question certain inclinations or possible predispositions that you might want to release, or at least modify. No doubt we all have had experiences with people who influenced us in a negative way, or at least a way with which we are not completely comfortable. Maybe they have a continued hold on our emotions, thoughts, or habits. If we can identify where those thoughts or actions came from, and visualize an alternative, we might feel more in control of our own fate. Sometimes, a negative influence has just been introduced into your work world and you want to be cautious of the impact they could have on you. Just be aware, continue to keep the important and valuable examples in your head, and keep control over the effect others have on you.

▶ UNDERSTAND HOW OTHERS VIEW YOU AND WHY IT MATTERS

Knowing how others view you is an important piece of self-awareness. Although it is not always a comfortable reality, especially for leaders striving to have loyal followers and collaborative colleagues, it can be helpful. Often, leaders oversee companies, communities, or schools with large numbers of constituents, employees, or residents. Because of that, many people in the organization do not get the time or opportunity to get to know the leader in a meaningful way. They may have never had the opportunity to have a one-on-one conversation, work with the leader in a team or committee, or interact with them informally or socially. Therefore, people rely on the leader's image or reputation to make judgments and determine their own level of loyalty, and whether they will align themselves.

This is often the case with parents, employees, colleagues, and the community in large school districts. People watch the leader's behavior and communication often from a distance. They might be watching you speak at a large public event or noticing how you walk into a room and interact with others. Other times, they are watching you online or in your social media posts or blogs. All those things constitute an image you are presenting, which certainly does not provide the totality of who you are; however, it must suffice when you do not have the time or the means to personally get to know everyone in the community.

Many school administrators, especially after being in the profession for several years, can relate to meeting someone who says, "I know you; I used to work for you," or "I remember you interviewed me 20 years ago." School leaders who stay in the same state or region find this occurrence a lot since many more people likely know you than you know them. It affirms the fact that how you come across, in every situation, in passing, up close, or even at a distance, can contribute to your long-term reputation. Some administrators will recall times when past employees have come to them and said things like, "I never knew you very well but I always appreciated the way you stopped to listen to people," or "I recall that every time you came into our school you seemed so happy to be there, and interested in what was going on." There might be other times when someone says something like, "All I remember is when you were in our district, people were afraid of you." That one is hard to swallow, but worth considering.

While this can have a lot to do with a title (like assistant superintendent for human resources) and the role you play (investigations and terminations in part), it can also have a lot to do with how you interact with people when you show up. What is your non-verbal communication? Do you reach out to the people you pass? Do you show interest in the students and staff? Did you hold the door for someone else or step in front of them? All of these behaviors influence how people talk about you to others and think about you as a leader.

Fair or unfair, right or wrong, the way you approach others, communicate in person and in writing, post, respond, and dress will come together to make an impression on others. I realized later in my career that there were a few decisions I made early on that made distinct impressions to others. Maybe I knew that would happen, maybe not. I cannot remember really thinking through it. At that point in my life, I probably would have said I did not care what others thought. Before I tell you the decisions, you should be aware of the context because these examples would not have had the same effects in a different part of the country (I was in the Midwest) or time period (this started in the 1990s).

One decision I made was to cut my hair very short. I realized along the way that some people had an impression of women with very short haircuts. That, coupled with an assertive personality, high energy, and a position of authority, i.e., school administrator, caused some to have the feeling that I was strict and unforgiving. Right or wrong, I was told along the way that the physical impression I gave was "harsh," "edgy," and "controlling." I wonder how much of that had to do with my physical appearance, how much had to do with my title, and more important, how much of it had to do with my behavior. Whatever it was, it is good to be aware of how others viewed me, because it impacted their level of anxiety and sometimes willingness or lack thereof to share openly with me in a serious conversation. Whether it is hairstyle or something else, knowing the overall impression you give can help you make subsequent decisions about appearance, behavior, communication, and your digital impression.

Second, I chose not to change my name when I married my husband in 1996. While it is much more common now, at that time and in that region, it was not common. It was different. It caused some people to make judgments about me. People in my school community commented about it, asking why I did not change my name. The most common question asked was, "Did your husband get mad?" If you knew my husband, that would make you laugh. I used to joke about not changing my name, saying that my husband and I have different last names because HE elected not to change his name when we got married. Some found that humorous, others did not. Again, right or wrong, it gave an impression, and my subsequent joke about it further perpetuated people's feeling that I was perhaps excessively independent, opinionated, and outspoken.

All of this is being stated only to raise the awareness of school leaders about their image, the way you are seen. It should not be taken as a directive on how to dress, cut your hair, or what you choose to call yourself. We must all be honest about who we are, and as we discussed in the section in this book on purpose, our unique individuality and authenticity help guide us to and through a more meaningful career. I am only suggesting that as you think about each decision you make around your appearance, behavior, communication, and digital presence consider if that is how you want others to see you.

An example of this for me would be that at times I can be very sarcastic to my detriment. While my intent is to be funny, connect, and lighten the mood, it can sometimes be harmful depending on the relationship and if I am not careful. This is an image consideration I have pondered and try to be conscientious about as I interact with others. Being sarcastic to the point that it is unkind is never my plan, nor would I ever want to give that impression. Making sure there is correlation between how you present yourself, and who you really are, is the point of this discussion. It is also important to think about how you want others to view you and how that might hurt or help your connections, communications, and leadership moving forward.

> Sometimes we make decisions or present in ways that are not truly aligned with our true character, or intent, and we come across to people differently than what we hoped.

Knowing the implications of how you present is worth pondering. Awareness, alignment, and authenticity are the sole reasons for this discussion.

There is another big piece to this topic that should not be left silent, and that is the part of our image that we do not control, yet others judge. Unfortunately, people make decisions about us, even when we have no control or choice over that part of our appearance, such as height, body shape, race, or hair texture to name a few. No doubt, some who read the section about image will automatically think about things around their appearance, which they do not control, and how others unfairly judge them because of deeply held prejudice or bias. This has been explored and discussed in depth by people for decades with credence given to the injustice certain individuals face regularly. These conversations among our educational leaders must continue as we share experiences and find ways to embrace and understand one another, as well as our own attitudes and viewpoints toward others.

As a general summary about image, the part you can control about your appearance, behavior, communication, and digital footprint is this. Now that I am on the other end of my career journey, I ask myself, "If I had to do it over, would I have made different decisions about my hairstyle, my last name, or any of the thousands of decisions I made in my 30's and 40's?" The answer is yes and no. I would do mostly what I did, all over again. I like being Patty Corum, my hair is still short. As for the consequences of the other choices I made in the first few decades of adult life, I am happily living with them. That being said, I would have benefited from realizing the impact on how some things, like a snappy sense of humor, coupled with other things, like a very driven personality and strong presence, came across to others.

By understanding it, naming it, and realizing certain effects, I probably would have made some revisions to my behavior earlier in my career. I would have slowed down a little, stopped to listen to others to a greater extent, and smiled more, maybe to compensate for my forceful nature. Mostly, I would have done those things because it would have resulted in better connection with others, others feeling more comfortable around me, more meaningful conversations, healthier success, and enhanced peace of mind. Fortunately, at some point, I learned the lessons before my career as a school administrator ended, and I have benefited from continuing to adjust my actions; but as will be true forever, I still have work to do.

▶ TAKE CARE OF YOU

We all know how important it is to take care of ourselves, and if we are not well, it is difficult to focus on and care for others. Leaders whose job it is to support, supervise, and grow other adults must first be self-aware enough to know their own wellness and how they plan to attend to their health needs on a regular basis. There are lots of ways to think about our own well-being. In this section, we will walk through different areas of wellness with examples of how educational leaders can concentrate on each. As we review, we will consider your lives as school leaders and remember that school administration is full of emotional drain, physical exhaustion, and occupational questioning. It leaves little time for social recreation and spiritual reset. There are ways to do it, and the better you are at incorporating your own wellness into your daily routine, the better you will be able to serve others. You will also feel better doing it.

We know that setting lofty goals as in New Year's resolutions often fails because people do not change their daily habits and routines. Whether is it exercising, eating healthy, taking breaks to breathe and recharge, and even communication habits like being a more careful and active listener, our daily behaviors are what shape our lives. We are often told to focus on what we do routinely because that is how we reach goals and make changes. Self-care as well as good communication are both something we can practice daily, and if we focus with intention, we can change outcomes in our lives. Exercising one day will not make an overall difference in how you feel, but exercising on a regular basis will. Being emotionally stable and demonstrating control over your feelings and responses are things that should be habitual, not just something you do every once in a while. As a school leader, you are so busy doing a thousand other things, you might wonder when you have time to focus on taking care of yourself.

As an administrator, there are many things that hit you daily, things that you are not expecting. One thing you can expect, however, is that many unexpected things will hit you daily! You are likely dealing with hundreds of children, dozens of adults, and critical responsibilities that include people's education, livelihood, and even safety. You are aware that your work can involve serious situations, strong emotions, and sometimes dire consequences. Knowing that your purpose is to support, supervise, and grow other adults, among other things, means you must be present, knowledgeable, confident, and alert at all times. As you consider bringing your best self to school every day, consider what that means.

> In my experience, the best and most successful school leaders are people who take care of themselves.

Daily, they spend time, although not necessarily a lot of time, in activities that focus on wellness. They not only concentrate on physical care, but also emotional, spiritual, social, intellectual, and occupational wellness (National Wellness Institute, 2025). They have spent some time upfront considering these domains and making plans to incorporate healthy habits into their daily routines. Subsequently, they spend time on a regular basis assessing their progress and their overall health. The habits they instill may be small, but powerful. After all, impact comes with consistency.

As we discuss each domain think about the small things you can incorporate into your daily schedule that might help you feel and be your best self. Write them down. Post them somewhere where you will see them every day. Display visual reminders, like placing your water bottle next to the sink, putting your tennis shoes by the door, using an app to remind yourself to pause and breathe, scheduling things like meditation and time with happy friends. In summary, think first about why each domain is important and what it means to you. Write down your plans to incorporate small behaviors into your daily routine. Writing them down helps ensure your commitment to implementation. Then do it. You will not be perfect, but you can make small steps. Finally, find a way to document your successes and be sure to give yourself credit for your progress.

▶ Physical Wellness

The most obvious place to start is your physical wellness, defined as "The consistent prioritization of physical self-care and the engagement in a variety of health-enriching behaviors"

(National Wellness Institute, 2025). Our jobs as school leaders can be very tiring, but think about the opportunities it gives you to incorporate good physical habits. You have the opportunity to have water at your desk. You have lots of steps you can take each day by visiting classrooms and walking through the building. You might have health insurance that provides for medical care when needed. Take advantage of all those things. Think about the chances you have to take care of your physical self, instead of the constraints because of your busy schedule. I remember that being an elementary principal seemed to leave little time for me to eat lunch, so I would snack instead, and then eat a big, unhealthy dinner. As an assistant superintendent, I thought I was much too busy to stop for lunch, but I had plenty of time to consume massive amounts of chocolate and coffee at my desk while working. I had control over all of that, but I relinquished that control to tasks and other people who I felt were demanding my time and attention. Ultimately it was up to me and for years, I made bad choices.

About mid-career, I figured out how differently I felt with just a few simple changes. I drank sparkling water instead of diet coke; I brought a healthy lunch that tasted good and did not give me a sugar high; I made time to walk daily, even if only a mile or two; and I figured out how to get the best sleep, even though it might not have been as many hours as I would have hoped. I started feeling better every day. I felt more alert, stronger, and happier. You do not have to be perfect and you do not have to run marathons, but taking the time to do even small things that you know make you feel physically better is worth it, and if you do it regularly, it will pay off every single day.

Why is physical self-care important to you? Do you feel differently when you make a conscious effort to eat better, sleep the right amount, exercise, and so on? It can be as simple as setting your alarm five minutes earlier to spend time stretching each morning or spending 20 minutes reading a good book before sleep, rather than looking at your email. How might that change your attitude? How might it change how your body feels? What you decide to do does not have to take a lot of time. A 20- or 30-minute walk, four or five times a week will matter! Once you start, you will not want to stop. Once it is a habit, you will feel strange if you do not do it.

▶ Emotional Wellness

Emotional wellness is defined as "The awareness and acceptance of one's feelings and the capacity to manage behaviors related to one's emotional state" (National Wellness Institute, 2025). Similarly, equanimity is "evenness of mind or temper; the quality or condition of being undisturbed by elation, depression, or agitating emotion; unruffledness" (Oxford University Press, n.d.). As we consider our emotional wellness, think about your mental serenity, steadiness, and composure, especially in a difficult situation. Evenness of mind and temper allows us to navigate the many curveballs that life and leadership throws, with grace and poise. This is an ancient virtue. Think of it as a state of mind that we can develop as we seek to enhance our inner sense of peace and how we react to the world around us. Emotional intelligence is another way to think about the capacity we have to understand, control, and express our emotions and handle relationships with regulation and empathy. It is the ability to manage your own emotions as well as understand the emotions of others. Equanimity and emotional intelligence are qualities you may have found in successful school leaders. They probably either have the innate trait to control their emotions, stay calm in crisis, and respond with empathy and self-regulation, or they have developed that trait over the years. For educational leaders, emotional wellness is an attribute worth practicing and enhancing, as others are watching your ability to lead with mature consideration and composure.

> School leaders have a lot of reasons to be emotionally healthy. First, we will not survive if we cannot self-regulate during all that happens in our jobs.

Leaders who bounce from one crisis to another with no regularity or self-control, usually do not see problems all the way through to resolution and often do not last long in their role. You watch them get frazzled, show extreme and irrational emotions, feel downtrodden, and blame others, which then results in unhealthy behaviors such as bad leadership decisions or poor health choices. It is easy to get into a downward spiral when we are unable to control our own emotions. For me, in my many years as an educational leader, my emotional stability seemed to be the most obvious one that I needed to control. I knew how it made me feel when I got extremely irritated with others because of their behavior, or when I felt so frayed, I could barely attend to the things and people in my areas of responsibility. It is a horrible feeling to be so anxious. Through several stressful situations, I realized my emotional self must be attended to if I was going to be a successful school leader. I knew it was up to me.

A second reason school administrators must pay attention to their emotional health is because others are watching. As a building principal, you set the tone for the school. You model the expectations of how we, as professionals, will respond to situations. You provide guidance for those who are seeking it. You teach others how to handle stressful situations with composure and calm. This, among other things, is your job as the leader. As you handle situations, especially in a crisis, think about what it would look like if everyone in the school responded the way you did. Would that be a good thing or not a good thing? Are you proud of how you approach different circumstances? Are your behaviors and attitudes helpful? Do they lead to good resolution or more chaos?

▶ Spiritual Wellness

Spiritual wellness is thought of differently by different people, but can be simply described as connecting with something greater than yourself. Defined as "The development of and appreciation for the depth and expanse of life and natural forces that exist in the universe" (National Wellness Institute, 2025), people who practice spiritual well-being may find meaning and motivation by identifying a noble commitment, something bigger than the here and now. It usually helps define our morals and values and gives us direction and hope. Many educational leaders credit their ability to stay focused, empathetic, and regulated at work to their overall spiritual principles.

Having a sense of spiritual well-being can include practices and engagement in religious communities and groups, spending time in meditation or prayer, participating in activities to help your community, or spending time embracing nature, people, and service to others. As an educational leader, your ability to think more broadly, have a larger perspective, and believe in meaning beyond immediate space and time can help you empathize with others, assess situations with more understanding and perspective, and be able to notice the difference between right and wrong and act accordingly. At work, it helps us recognize the differences in important, mildly important, and unimportant.

> Having a broader perspective helps us to categorize and prioritize our world and our work so we are not spinning our wheels and investing unnecessary time in meaningless endeavors.

Spiritual wellness provides guidance for a focus on others and a goal of living with peace and harmony. It helps you link your purpose in life to your commitment as an educational leader.

Most educators in my experience believe that becoming a teacher, a principal, or anyone working in a school for that matter is a response to a higher calling to help others. When talking with teachers and principals, you will often hear them say they love having a hand in helping a child learn to read, providing opportunities where children grow socially and emotionally, or simply working in a position that allows them to serve others. You will often identify and describe happy and successful educators as altruistic, generous, benevolent, and other-centered. This could be a part of their overall inherent belief that they have been called to do something meaningful and powerful for others.

▶ Intellectual Wellness

Typically, educational leaders are well adept in intellectual wellness, defined as "The creative, stimulating activities that lead to learning, personal growth, and the sharing of one's unique gifts with others" (National Wellness Institute, 2025). Because the job itself requires constant learning and developing, we seem to be constantly formulating mental and intellectual pursuits. This involves engaging in activities that challenge our brains, develop critical skills, and explore new ideas. If you are in your first few years in school administration you are likely, constantly exposing yourself to fresh perspectives, novel approaches, and out-of-the-box thinking. You are forced to meet new people, understand new ideas, and study the things you do not yet know.

Leaders who sometimes need to pay more attention to their intellectual well-being are those who have been in the profession for years and may think they have little more to learn. Although I believe this kind of thinking is rare in educational leadership, it may happen that someone has decided not to pursue continued development. This is when problems begin to happen and others in the community pray for their retirement, even though their longevity may be appreciated. Although, as we age and undoubtedly have more knowledge and experience than we did in years past, intellectual stimulation continues to be essential.

▶ Social Wellness

Social wellness is your social functioning, and the ability to build healthy, meaningful relationships, and genuinely care about the people around you. It means being able to manage conflict, set boundaries, and understand yourself and how you relate to others. It is defined by National Wellness Institute (2025) as "The contribution to one's environment and community with an emphasis on the interdependence between others and nature." Think about how you interact with others at work. Do you accept and believe in people around you to be able to contribute? Are you comfortable spending time with others? Do you feel good when you are around them? Do you believe they and you are vital members of the community who provide meaningful contributions? These are just a few questions to ponder.

Healthy social interactions are essential to leadership. A large part of your responsibilities includes building relationships, understanding, and working with others, and getting the most out of your team while maintaining the trust and confidence others have in you. You need them because you cannot do it alone. It is your job to inspire development, motivation, and hard work in others. Successful administrators do not shy away from employees or community members, the easy ones, or the challenging ones. They embrace people and discover ways to capitalize on others' strengths and possible contributions. They are hopeful and they recognize potential in others and in the organization.

Now, if you tend to be more reserved, the thought of being expected to interact regularly may not be easy, even dreadful at times. You may not relish the thought of a big social event, making small talk, or constantly being bombarded with people approaching you. Some of the best leaders I know are introverts. They prefer time alone and will choose opportunities for solitude over social interactions and cajoling. The introverted leaders I am thinking about appear to have great relationships with others; however, because I know them personally, I realize they would often rather be alone than mixed up in the pandemonium that comes with constant contact with others. Of course, there is no right or wrong to being an introvert versus an extrovert, and great educational leaders come in both categories.

The key is knowing who you are and how to use all your traits to your advantage and to the advantage of others. Since human interactions are important to leadership, if you tend to be more reticent, remember to get what you need! Be wise, and carve out time daily to spend with yourself, your planning, thinking, and reflecting. Use the strength you gather from that alone time to approach others with confidence. Embrace the opportunity for interaction, because you know the importance of conversations and relationships, and what they mean to others. Your interaction with them is a gift, and typically, they want as much of you as they can get. Think of the wisdom you have because you spend time in reflection and thought, and use that to model for and listen to others. Whether you tend to be more reserved or more outgoing, you can use your strengths to serve others.

Another way to think about social wellness is to have and maintain a supportive network of people you can rely on when you need help. Different people in our lives interact with us in different ways and as you think about what you find most helpful and supportive, who are those folks? Typically, the best critical friends are those who will listen thoroughly, understand your message and your emotions, and help guide you to a healthy outcome. Sometimes they just listen to provide a place for you to work through your dilemma yourself. Other times, they have suggestions or insight, based on knowing you, your values, and goals. Either way, they have your best interest in mind. They care about you, uplift you and remind you of your value and your strength. These are important people to have around, especially as a leader.

When life is at its busiest, outings we find to be fun and enjoyable with family and friends seem to take a backseat. As you think about self-care, consider the weight of this one, especially as a school leader. It is important to spend time, in and out of work hours, with people you choose, and people you find uplifting. What do you enjoy? With whom? Who makes you laugh, helps you find peace, and reminds you of the things you love? Try to spend time with those people on a regular basis. The pleasure we receive from spending time being entertained or having fun can last longer than just the hours we invest. It reminds us who we are and what we have to offer. It prompts us to think about our interests, as well as people we love and how generous life can be.

Developing a sense of connection with others, being at peace with who we are and what we bring to the gathering, and developing a positive support system are all healthy things to do. Although we seem to have little extra time as administrators, I would argue that time spent on considering how you interact with others, and who you spend time with, has an important impact on your peace of mind. Think about the way you feel after spending time with someone in a conversation that went well, after a problem was solved by teamwork, or being with someone who believes in you and fills your bucket. When you leave, you feel uplifted, inspired, and recharged. To me, a long-time educational leader, that is social wellness.

▶ Occupational Wellness

For some, constantly debating the decision to be a school administrator seems to be a common practice. Some leaders do it all the way through their careers. If you are questioning yourself and your choices, and at the same time trying to perform as best you can, it might feel like a constant struggle. You could be feeling like you are working with one foot inside the organization and one foot searching for something else. This alone can make work even more stressful. Why do some school leaders constantly question their choice to be a school administrator? I think the answer is this. It is a difficult and important job that has tremendous implications for the staff, families, and children we serve. How can you find peace with your decision, and balance in your life as you fill the demanding role of administration? National Wellness Institute, 2025 defines vocational wellness as

"The personal satisfaction and enrichment one receives in life through their employment, academic, or volunteer work."

First, let's talk about why the role of school administration is so strenuous. Depending on your exact position, you are ultimately responsible for something exceptionally valuable – children. If your job is not directly in a school, and you are the director of a department, like technology or food service, you are still serving students, and your ability to do it well contributes to the overall success of children's educational experiences. If you are a principal or assistant principal, you are working with children every day, and it is your absolute responsibility to supervise and hold accountable all that is happening in your school so that students have a positive, productive experience. Even though you cannot control the choices the employees make, you are responsible for what they do and how they do it, when children are involved. You are ultimately responsible for a quality, safe, and meaningful educational experience for every student in that school.

The adults we supervise are not necessarily ones we would have chosen if given the opportunity. They can be complicated. The parents of the children are fully invested because we have their children for many hours a day. They can be emotional and needy, which is completely understandable. In addition to our immediate school community, we usually never fully agree with all policies and practices in the district. There may be administrators above you, who in your opinion make poor decisions or are not good leaders. So, you are stuck in the middle of bosses, school boards, parents, and employees all pulling in different directions. Add to that, the social and political influences that currently plague our school leaders everywhere. Let it be said in no uncertain terms, this is a demanding space to occupy.

So, how do we respond? Some school administrators simply become stuck in negativity and blame. They continually find reasons to be disgruntled. They find it hard to find hope, do their work with purpose, or lead in positive and constructive ways. They bring others down with them and eventually find they are working in a community of pessimism and disapproval. The culture and climate are strikingly impacted, good employees leave to go to more positive and stable schools, and district office leaders begin to question the performance and effectiveness of such administrators. This is a grim description; however, it is one way people respond to the life of school administration.

Another way administrators respond to feelings of dissatisfaction is to find another school district. This might be a productive step; however, you should be aware that, well, you know the saying, the grass is not always greener on the other side! Sometimes when moving from one district to another, you simply swap one set of problems for another. Of course, sometimes if the fit is not right in your first position, this is a valuable move; however, if it is a pattern to constantly be looking for another home that will suit you better, consider this. The harmony you are seeking may not come from another district. It starts with you.

Finally, we must talk about work/life balance. How much time are you willing to spend in work activities? What sacrifices are you prepared to make for your job? How will you balance your obligations for the career, and the other things you choose in life like family, friends, personal time, self-care, and social connectedness? These are all considerations as you ponder your choices about school administration. When you sign up to take responsibility for other people's children, you may be subsequently signing up to relinquish time spent with your own family. What will that look like? Are you willing to do that?

> In my journey, as I considered changing districts from time to time, I found it helpful to keep in mind the immensity of the job, no matter where it was, and realize the fact that my happiness comes from me, not from external sources, like bosses, colleagues, employees, policies, or communities.

▶ Summary of Wellness

Contemplating your own overall wellness and incorporating activities so that you are your best can be extremely helpful to school administrators. Because of the complexity and pressures of the job, your wellness will no doubt add to your ability to hold up in difficult times. Self-care takes commitment, and you must remember that it is not only our physical and emotional health we have to consider, but it also includes things like social, spiritual, intellectual, and occupational wellness. It is not selfish to think about how you will take care of yourself, every single day. If you are unwell or unregulated, it will show in your leadership, and you could be a less effective school administrator, even a detriment to the organization. It can also impact the way you feel about yourself, and how content and satisfied you are with your work and your life.

▶ EMBRACE YOUR CONTROL AND LET GO OF THE REST

People of all kinds are everywhere and as a long-time adult, I can say this for certain; I have found some adults are extremely pleasing to work with, while others can be straight up irritating. I find some people to be calm, kind, and comfortable in a conversation. Others might feel much the opposite to me, grating and aggravating. Perhaps you have the same reactions in your experiences. And in all my decades spent with others, I have come to know one thing. After resisting this notion for years, I finally get it. Other successful leaders have pointed it out, but now I can grasp what they were trying to tell me. Even my mom and dad taught me this lesson from the very beginning of my life. It took me a while to get there, but now, I understand.

> The irritation is mine. The frustration lives in me and is actually because of me, not them.

As I am sitting there feeling annoyed, judging their actions, thinking about rolling my eyes, and making an exit plan in my head, I realize it now. The other person is probably feeling none of those emotions. In fact, I really have no idea what emotions they are feeling because I am not listening. I am just adjudicating and focusing on my discernment. They are talking and I am miserable. I cannot escape my thoughts about how they should do something different, or be different. Whatever it is, it is grating on every nerve. And they seem to be so at ease with their know-it-all attitude, self-serving rant, or whatever it is that seems to be bothering me that day. I stay engaged in my thoughts about how much I dislike them or what they stand for. For some conversations, it is not that bad; it might be a mere thought in my mind, "Why can't they be different?"

This is what happens when we focus on the things we cannot control, when we allow someone else to affect us in such a profound way. It sounds odd when you think about it, but how many nights have we lost sleep, perseverating on things for which we have absolutely no control? For some of us, too many to count. And what good does it do? The lesson is an important one for educational leaders. We are responsible for so many things, things that rightfully cause us to spend hours considering the issues and what to do next. Why in the world would we rob ourselves of time over things about which we can do nothing? The final section in this chapter, and maybe the one that can save us the most time and heartache, is about what we control, what we do not control, and what we can do about it.

▶ A Personal Introduction

About three decades ago, when my husband and I had been dating for a few months, I said to him, "You make me so happy."

He went on to tell me it wasn't HE who "made me happy." He noticed early in our relationship, I seemed to be a cheerful, optimistic person, and that he enjoyed being around me. That was powerful, and it stuck with me to this day. And he was right. I own my happy. I own my mad. I own my peace. I own my frustration. The more I have grown to understand

> I will never forget his response. He said, "I do not have the power to make you happy. You make yourself happy, and that is what I like about you."

what is within my power and control, and what is not, the more content I am, the more focused on my work and my life and the better I am to myself and other people. Thank you, Brent, for that reminder, early in my leadership career. And thank you for continuing to be a significant part of the happiness I possess.

▶ Understand Your Control

From the beginning of our time on earth, we learn the power of control. The words, "I can do it," start as early as age 1 or 2, when a child is exploring their first attempts at language and power. They want to feed themselves, hold the crayon, and use the scissors. Even before their hands and minds can navigate the tools, they want to oversee their own situation. As teachers, parents, and grandparents, we know that the sooner we let them do it themselves, as soon as it is safe of course, the more interested they are, and the faster they master the concept. They feel empowered and successful. Of course, as children grow, the desire to control things moves from crayons and feeding, to decisions about what to wear, after-school activities, and friendships. It does not end there. Graduate students ask for control over their assignments, timelines, and methods of learning. Employees want the ability to make decisions about their work hours, location of work, personal leave, and schedules.

As adults and as leaders, we might not spend enough time contemplating the whole notion of control. As an adult, having control over things in our lives is so inherent, we may take it for granted. Understanding control for school leadership should be considered every day, and in every interaction. In trying to solve problems, thinking about the next steps, planning, and connecting with others, it will do you well to constantly think about what you control, what you do not control, what is within your area of responsibility, and all the choices you have and do not have, in taking your next steps.

After watching great leaders not only tolerate, but also embrace whatever and whoever comes their way with acceptance and dignity, I learned these great leaders started with sincere introspection. What I decided was that I needed to own my reactions when it came to responding to other people and events, things over which I have no control.

It comes from within me, not you. There are certainly times when it is harder to control our reactions to the outside world; however, the more we can focus on the fact, we have no control over others, and we have lots of control over ourselves, the more in charge we can be. Now, what?

> The exasperation I was feeling was coming from my attitude, my perspective, my judgments. You cannot irritate me without my permission. That emotion is mine.

How do we deal with ourselves when we tend to get out of sorts because of someone else's behavior? It helps to own the emotion. If you do not believe it is yours and it is within your control, then it will be hard to do anything about it. After all, you are not going to change the other person who is exhibiting the behaviors that are bothering you. So, own your reactions, and believe that you are the only one who can do anything with them. Then what? Do you let it sit there? Try to change it? What if you relish the irritation? (It seems like sometimes we somehow enjoy spending time being bothered by others.) If you want to stop giving that person the time and space in your head, how do you let go?

One thing to do is to consider the fact that some behaviors bother some people but do not bother other people. One individual at Thanksgiving, for example, was highly offended by what someone else wore to the occasion. Others at the same gathering, no doubt did not even notice and were certainly not bothered. In their minds, someone else's appearance was of no concern to them. To the person concerned, the dress was highly inappropriate, so much so, they wanted to comment and advise the person they should not wear that in the future. Along the same lines, some drivers get uptight in traffic, some to the point they yell and make gestures to other drivers. Others turn up the radio, consider it part of living and driving, and continue without much emotional or physical reaction. When that happens to one friend of mine, she actually repeats out loud, "I care about you. I hope you are ok. I am sending positive vibes your way."

Let us not forget the control we ultimately have over how we think about things and subsequently, the behaviors we exhibit. While I may find your choices in pizza toppings despicable, for example, when it comes down to it, it really does not matter what I think about whether you choose peperoni or mushrooms. Sometimes, in certain circumstances, it might be helpful to comment, make judgment, and advise, but certainly not every time. Start by examining the situation that is bothering you. Is it upsetting to a large number of people? Does it cause harm? Is it disruptive or merely objectionable to you? Simply think about the fact that we all have judgments and we might be well served, before we act to ponder the benefits of sharing those opinions, or simply keeping them to ourselves.

Besides realizing that your opinion is just that, your opinion, we should also consider the power we have over the situation, and if in fact, this situation is within our control or frankly none of our business. For example, what someone else wears to someone else's Thanksgiving dinner is not something that you would typically control. You are not the host. It is not your house and you are not in charge of dressing people, no matter how unacceptable you find it. So why get involved? If you do not have the power to do something about it, let it go. It is not yours. "But I feel the need to say something," you might think. Ok, but how will that change the situation? Will the person dress differently next time? Probably not. In fact, they might double down on their distasteful choice. Will you feel better? Maybe, and maybe not. Will there be fallout with other guests? Probably. Some will side with you; others will say it is none of your business and suddenly, the focus shifts from green bean casserole and cranberry sauce to disagreement and catty gossip about what someone is wearing and the audacity of someone else to actually say something. All of that is up to you. Just consider, is this yours to deal with? And most importantly, what are your feelings doing to your own peace and happiness? Some people have enough trouble keeping themselves in line, so taking on the behaviors, attitudes, and appearance of others just might be a step too far.

At Thanksgiving dinner, for example, what kinds of choices do you have and can you demonstrate in that moment? You can probably sit wherever you like. Perhaps you decide to choose not to sit by the person with the distasteful (in your opinion) outfit. Maybe, on the other hand you decide you will actually sit by that person and try to get to know them better. Maybe you decide to work on your tolerance and listening skills as you sit with that person. Or perhaps you choose to sit next to someone you find funny so that you are sure to get some good laughs over turkey and dressing.

> Another way to deal with the annoying things that make their way into your headspace is to replace those thoughts of irritation with thoughts of the things you can control.

You control what you eat and what you drink. Focus on which goodies you will consume and savor every bite. You control those little bursts of conversations before and after dinner with people you enjoy. Seek those you find comforting and enjoyable. Catch up with them. Find out what they have been up to. You control how much you share and how much you listen. Enjoy the exchange. And, of course, you will ultimately determine when you decide to leave. It is much more pleasing to think about the things we control than to perseverate on the things we do not control. We can find peace and resolution when we exhibit the power we have.

As a school leader, contemplating your control over yourself and your emotions is important. Why? People are watching you. You are dealing with serious situations and your leadership could impact how the entire community moves forward. If you get rattled by every other person's idiosyncrasy, it will be difficult to lead with perspective and wisdom. Should you get caught up in the minutia of every detail of someone else's choices, your focus on the mission and vision of the school could be disrupted. The examples above about Thanksgiving outfits, traffic, and pizza are examples to get you thinking about how sometimes we tend to become so engrossed in other people's choices, and it takes us away from the tremendous control we must have to lead happy lives and work in productive ways. Too much immersion in things you cannot control can keep you from focusing on you, your purpose, your goals in leadership and life, and the work of building culture, and developing educators. It can also inhibit you from finding your own peace of mind.

This scenario illustrates what we have been discussing about control. It is about a colleague who resides in the business world.

TOM THE ANGRY TECH

A professional colleague who is a successful entrepreneur with many clients called me one day and said, "Patty I need your help. I have a difficult client and he is keeping me awake at night. In fact, I even contacted my doctor this morning because I thought I was having a panic attack. It's all because of him." I asked her to tell me what was going on. My colleague described the client, Tom, as a very aggressive person, who constantly disagrees with her suggestions on timelines and delivery models for their marketing. He often cusses at her and tells her how difficult she is making his job.

She decided to contact the president of the company, who told her to just ignore Tom. The president said he treats everyone like that and assured my colleague that the company trusted her to make the decisions. He said to disregard Tom when he acted in this manner. While he has a piece of the workload, ultimately, he has to do as he is told. That being said, Tom was still occupying a lot of time and headspace for my colleague and she continued to be infuriated by his behavior.

I suggested the phone call with the president of the company was a great idea and what he told her was wonderful news! She had permission of the person who had hired her to ignore Tom's demands. She was told to continue to communicate with Tom to make sure the work was getting done; however, she did not have to collaborate with him. Ultimately, she made the decisions.

Situations like this sometimes do not have the caveat that you are being supported by the higher-ups, and you can ignore the one that is making your life miserable. Still, she was infuriated and reported that Tom was making her anxiety escalate to the point she felt out of control. She knew it did not make sense that Tom was in her head and causing her so much anguish, but nonetheless, it was real. In trying to be nice and hear him out, she was beginning to doubt herself. Now he is impacting her sleep and her ability to focus on other things like her family and her own health.

We talked about her circle of control. I asked her to name all the things that she has control over in this situation. Ultimately, per the president of the company, she has control over the marketing decisions. She knew that. She appreciated the fact that she did not have to get Tom's approval on anything. So why was she so exasperated?

What she failed to realize is that in addition to authority over the work decisions, she also controls how long she chooses to listen to Tom on calls. She controls the words she says to him. She controls whether to stop the conversation because it is inappropriate and not productive. She understood she controls the work, despite his disagreements, but she forgot to think about the fact that more importantly, she also controls her attitudes about him, her reactions verbally and emotionally, how long she chooses to listen to him, what she says to him when she ends the non-productive calls, and finally, what she thinks about once she hangs up. When she lays in bed at night, she has so many things to choose to think about as a working mom with a supportive husband, two beautiful children, and a nice home; why does she let him take up so much of her headspace?

Our conversation was extremely eye-opening for her and reminded her that she is not forced to sit and listen to anyone who is talking to her so disrespectfully! She is also not required to think about him all evening and how much she despises his behavior. She responded, "Of course, why do I put myself through this? How have I let him control my mind?" She also realized that there is nothing she can do, no matter how many hours she decides to give him, that will change his attitudes and behaviors. He is who he is, so let it go! I suggested some language for her to use with him when he begins his rants.

"Tom, I am not going to listen to you berate me and cuss at me. If you have something to say in a professional way, I will listen, otherwise, I am hanging up and we will release the marketing on Tuesday."

OR

"Tom, if you can tell me your ideas without yelling at me, I have ten minutes. I will listen and consider them. Otherwise, I am ending this call and moving forward."

I also suggested to my colleague as thoughts of Tom and his irritating disposition enter your headspace at night replace them with something else. Say to yourself, "I am not going to give Tom any more of my time and thought today. I choose to think about my boys and the activities we have planned for tomorrow. They are going to be so excited when they see this new museum."

That is it. Simply exercise the control you have. Stop the conversation. Tell the person what you will and will not tolerate. Then tell yourself that Tom's behavior is outside your control. This is not about you. Then, do not give him the power to be in your valuable headspace, time, heart, and rest. That is yours. Protect it. Those people in your home you love, and your extended family and good friends all deserve your time and attention more than Tom. So stop letting him hijack your mind, and get on with the things that make you happy!

▶ Your Control and School Leadership

How, as school leaders, can we embrace the control we have, stop fretting over the things in which we have no control, and understand how effective school leaders use the power and influence they have to effectively manage a school and lead people? Let us first think about the notion of control. For a long time, effective teachers have known that if we give students choice in their topic for writing, choice in the way they want to solve a math problem, or choice in how they want to present a particular concept to the class, the chance of understanding and applying the learning increases, and the students tend to demonstrate more enthusiasm and initiative. Control is a powerful motivator. And control is important to people. We like it. We want it. Interestingly, we have more control than we sometimes use, but then at the same time, we agonize over things for which we have no control.

One reason to consider the concept of control as a school leader is to understand how much control we actually do have, so that we can use it. Sometimes, we find ourselves being controlled, rather than asserting our own control. In other words, we feel like other people or circumstances are making our decisions for us. We may have plans to work out before we go to school, for example, but someone calls and wants to know if we can swing by another school to pick up supplies for a district event. Realizing the extra time this is going to take, but wanting to help the other administrator, we skip the workout and go help. That decision is within your control.

> Embracing all that you control, and releasing the worry over all the things you cannot control is an extremely liberating and an important part of effective leadership and having meaningful conversations.

As you are contemplating your choices, remember, you have the control to do what you want. If you decide to skip your workout and help a colleague after considering everything, embrace it and remember, you chose to do it.

Think about the control that our cell phones and smart watches seem to have over us. We do not have to look at it when it vibrates, but we often do. We do not have to answer a text right away, especially when we are in the middle of a conversation with a student's parent, but sometimes we feel like we have no choice. And with that, our mind then wanders to the other situation, and our attention is officially diverted. The consideration we were once giving to one activity (our own wellness, or in the second example, another person) is sidetracked. The truth is, you have control. You made the decision to skip the workout. You made the decision to look at your phone or answer the text. And the subsequent results of your actions are felt by you and others, and have an impact on your capacity to connect and effectively communicate with others.

While we actually have a lot of choices in the life we live, and how we navigate work, communicate, and build relationships, we somehow let that control slip away as we try to please others and attend to everything at once. We may actually begin to feel that we are somewhat powerless in our lives. This is a slippery slope. In training with a group of department leaders in a school district, I asked them to make a list of all the things they control. The director of technology wrote only one word. When I asked her to report out, she said, "I wrote one word. 'Nothing.'" When asked to explain, she said she currently feels like everything in her life is decided by her children, her employer, the traffic, the weather, the economy, or her staff. She felt she was not in control of anything in her life. She said she felt like a puppet on strings, with other people controlling all of her movements and emotions.

That is not a good place to be! Feeling powerless can have multiple repercussions. She had become so distracted from following her own mission and vision, doing what she believed, and embracing her choices and her life, she ended up on paths she never wanted to be. We can't let that happen, especially as leaders. What a dreadful thought that you feel you control nothing in your life. In a different training I was conducting, also with school support staff directors, after giving the same prompt, list all the things you control, one individual also wrote only one word. But the word was different. When asked to report out, this food service director stated, "I wrote only one word and that is 'myself.'" When asked to explain, she began verbalizing everything she felt she had control over, including her actions, attitude, behaviors, thoughts, listening, responses, non-verbal communication, schedule, facial expressions, kindness, appreciation, judgments, values, faith, political views, and so on. She even listed the type of hair spray she used that morning and articulated the thought process she went through to make that decision. The point she was making, she has much control in her life, and she tries to recognize all of it. It just so happens; she was a successful and motivated school leader who continues to have loyal and happy followers.

We can thank Stephen R. Covey in *The 7 Habits of Highly Effective People*, who popularized a concept we can use to think about our power. This is a model which contains concentric circles named the circle of control (the innermost circle), circle of influence (between the other two circles) and circle of concern (the outside circle).

In the outermost concentric circle is the circle of concern, and this domain contains the things for which we have no control. This would include other people's words and actions, the economy, major world events, past happenings, and the weather to name a few. What Covey suggests is that these are the things we should spend little or no time agonizing over because they are things we cannot do anything about. Our worry and fuss will have no impact on the weather, for example, and we would be better served to consider the things we can control in the midst of extremely hot temperatures or major ice storms. We cannot direct the weather; however, we can choose what we wear.

The middle circle in Covey's model, the one between circle of control and circle of concern is called circle of influence. This one is more of a gray area, and it is comprised of those things we may have some influence over, albeit not full control. In relationships, for example, we do contribute to what happens between us and another person in terms of the decisions we make such as our energy, our language, our reactions, and our empathy. While we cannot control the other person and what they contribute or how they respond, our actions often influence them and influence our relationship one way or another. Another example would be our health. Although genetic make-up and outside forces can impact our wellness, we know that we can contribute to our well-being by eating healthy foods, exercising, and staying well emotionally and mentally. Ultimately, we cannot control our complete wellness; however, we are able to influence it through the decisions we make. This would also fall into that center circle of influence.

The innermost circle is the circle of control. For some, their circle of control is larger than others' because they have decided that they are in control of more things. These are people who believe in their control and take ownership of how they feel, behave, and react. These people believe their success and happiness is largely dependent upon them, their choices, their attitudes, and how they approach and view life and people. They are able to identify the many things for which they have power, and focus on that, rather than the things they do not control.

So, first, we want to understand control, because we want to be clear on the many things we have power over in our lives. When we do that, we are more inspired to seek solutions, more motivated to move forward, we see more options, and we feel more successful when things go well. We can give ourselves credit for the decisions we make based on the choices we have. When faced with a dilemma, it is a lot more empowering to realize the many options that are within our circle of control and contemplate each one to deliberately choose our next step. If, on the other hand, we spend all our time focusing on the things that upset us, personalities of others, or extrinsic stimuli we cannot control, we may find ourselves stuck. So first, know your control so that you know your options.

The second reason to understand your control as a school leader is the ability to let go of the things you do not control and release everyone else's "stuff." Letting go of the things you cannot control is liberating. Consider how you would feel if you could retrieve all the sleepless nights you spent worrying about things over which you had absolutely no control. And usually, when we ponder those lost hours, we realize not only did we lose valuable rest and time, it did not do any good to agonize, and it changed nothing in terms of whatever it was we were worried about. Think about the people who have hijacked your mind for hours or days, or possibly longer. Sometimes they are not even people who are important to us, we just allow them to get in our heads and drive us crazy! It would be nice if we could simply flip a switch. While there is no switch, there are ways to work on setting aside those persisting thoughts.

Try to give as much power to this thought as you do to the negative one about someone else. "They do not deserve my attention and time, and I am not going to think about it. Instead, I am going to think about something enjoyable, something I can handle, something I choose." Repeat this. "I cannot control that person and how they speak, or treat people. It is out of my lane. It is outside my circle of control. It does not deserve my valuable time and headspace." Then replace that thought with something you can control, like planning your weekend, thinking about your next fun project, or envisioning a celebration for someone you love.

▶ Control and Difficult Conversations

Using the control that you have as an educational leader can be extremely helpful in a difficult conversation. So often when having a sensitive conversation, the other person displays unappealing behaviors like becoming defensive, deferring, or making excuses. Consider a time you sat down to talk with someone and they completely derailed the conversation. In this scenario, remember the control you have as you navigate a dialogue with Ellen about her classroom space.

ELLEN THE EXCUSE MAKER

You are the assistant director in an early childhood center, and you have asked Ellen if you can speak with her about the extreme disorganization and number of materials piled in her classroom. Ellen has been teaching for many years and has acquired many books, games, manipulatives, experiments, resources, and even empty tubs, all of which she chooses to store in her classroom. Students have trouble moving from place to place, and there have even been a couple of mishaps where towers of books have fallen on students. While nobody has been injured, and

Ellen is a good teacher, you know that she needs to organize her space better to maximize learning for students, not to mention to ensure safety. It is starting to become a real problem. You and she have discussed this in passing, but never really had a conversation about the expectation that she begins to purge and organize. That is your purpose for this meeting. You plan on this being a simple conversation because you have established a good relationship with Ellen. What you did not plan for was that Ellen is going to have a hard time accepting your direction.

"Ellen, thank you for meeting with me today about your classroom. I am sure you put some thought to this since we set up this meeting last week. I wanted to meet today to hear about your plan to begin to make more space for your teaching, and see if there was anything I could do to assist. I know it is going to take some time, but I would like for you to start this week, and by the end of next week, we should see considerable difference. I know you'll be pleased once you do it. You have so many good activities for your kindergarteners and like we talked about last week, all the materials you have in that space are getting in the way."

Ellen responds, "Thanks. I have been thinking about this a lot since we talked. And I have a question for you. How come our classrooms don't have large storage closets? I have a lot of good stuff in there, and I do not have room at home to store it. When I asked about this before, you showed me one little bitty closet and said that was all the space you had. That isn't really acceptable. My friend works in a school district in another state where they have huge storage for every teacher. Why can't we have this?" Although her question is related to the topic, this is an example of Ellen deferring the main topic of the meeting. She quickly went from the need for her to clean out her classroom to her opinion that their school should have more storage for teachers. Here is your opportunity to exercise the control you have, to keep her on track.

"I understand, Ellen, and it would be nice if every classroom had a large storage area for everything, but we do not. Let's focus on when and how you are going to start making space. Would it make sense if our custodian comes down one day after school this week to help you move the things that are least important to your car or to the small closet, I showed you?"

Ellen has more ideas she wants to share before talking about her plan to clean. "I want to talk about how this other school did it. First, they had declining enrollment, like we do, and so they simply made class sizes a little bit larger so they could free up three classrooms where teachers could store their things. One was for primary teachers, one for intermediate and one for the specialists. Can I show you a map of how they did it?" Remember, you have control over this meeting. Stay focused.

"Not right now. Right now, I'd like for you and I to agree on a plan and a timeline for making more space in your classroom. The space for

> students is getting tighter and tighter and we need to solve this problem soon. I will help in any way I can, and you will need to make some decisions about where you will go with your materials. What day this week would you like for our custodian to come and help?"
>
> Ellen may continue to try to deflect the problem; however, since you have a clear purpose for the meeting, and the outcome has been stated, you will continue to reiterate it until a plan has been made. This is well within your area of control. Do not allow her to hijack the conversation. You can simply stop her and remind her about why you are meeting.

This is just one example of the control we have in conversations, and in this book, you will continue to learn other ways to exercise the power you have in messy situations.

▶ I Cannot Control Them, but I Am Responsible for Them

This is the hard part for leaders, administrators, bosses, people who are responsible for the supervision of other adults. While we cannot control other people, we have signed up to take responsibility for them, their actions and the education and other services they provide to children and to the school community. Perhaps after reading the first part of this section, you have decided you like the idea of letting go of the things you cannot control. Now, as a school leader, you must consider the fact that while you cannot control the adults in your school community, you are responsible for them and their conduct. Here are some thoughts to ponder regarding school leadership and control.

> *Effective leadership is about influencing and inspiring others to be the best they can be, not controlling people.*
>
> *We cannot control employees in our schools, yet there are certain job expectations for which we are expected to hold them to account.*
>
> *As the school administrator, how do I decide what is within my responsibility and control, and what is completely outside of my circle of control and I need to simply let go?*

▶ *Effective Leadership Is about Influencing and Inspiring Others to Be the Best They Can Be, Not Controlling People*

The best school leaders are those who can inspire and encourage others to think for themselves, do the right thing, continuously reflect and grow in their professional journey and even personal endeavors, and ultimately be great leaders themselves. Think of people who have had the greatest impact on you. They probably did not tell you what to do, instead, through their ability and willingness to listen to, understand, relate, pay attention to, and trust you to do the right thing, they inspired you to be a great leader yourself.

Fortunately, educators work in communities where people tend to enjoy interactions with others, care about the education of children, and crave teamwork and inclusivity. You will find many natural leaders in school environments, people who have the capacity to do great things and teach others. Remember that, and expect to see great things from the people with whom you work. Influence in leadership starts with being authentic, knowledgeable, hardworking, and confident. Be the caring person who is willing to listen, understand, and trust others to do great work. Inspirational leaders typically have positive presuppositions about others, which may be your first and most powerful way to inspire them.

▶ *We Cannot Control Employees in Our Schools, Yet There Are Certain Job Expectations for Which I Am Expected to Hold Them to Account*

Going back to the previous discussion about what someone wore to Thanksgiving dinner, now let us place that scenario into an educational setting, where a teacher wears an outfit you believe is distasteful and inappropriate for the school setting. You are the principal, which makes you responsible for implementing and enforcing policy, as well as making sure employees execute good judgment around students. Sometimes, it is clear. Perhaps there is a dress code policy in the district which states what employees can and cannot wear on school days. If that is the case, you can refer to the policy and expect the teacher to follow that directive. If, however, there is no written policy and you have learned that there is little precedent in the school about a dress code, this situation becomes more unclear. If employees have always dressed casually, and school and district administrators have never taken a hard line on what employees choose to wear, unless it is something drug or alcohol related, then what are you to do?

First, think about your responsibility as the school leader. Does the dress of an employee fall in your job description? Most school leaders would say yes, if it is negatively impacting the environment and/or children, or if it is against district policy. In this case, if it is not against policy, however in your mind, you feel it could be negatively impacting the educational environment, then you have a responsibility to do something. Is it causing disruption? Is it a distraction to learning? Think about what control you have in this situation. If it is not against policy, however you believe it is distracting, do you have the authority to require the person to refrain from wearing the outfit again? You might want to get advice, at some point, from a trusted colleague in the district, or a district administrator. If the district administrator tells you that in other cases, the district has not taken a stand on that particular item of clothing, and other teachers are allowed to wear it, then you might think about one of two options. One would be to try to change the thinking of the district if you feel strongly that there is disruption due to this particular item of clothing. Bring your justification and discuss it with the people who have the authority to make changes in policy. Or, if you feel it is of little consequence, drop it.

This is one example and is provided so that you think about the control you do have and the control you do not have. Other examples can include things that are far more serious and timelier, like safety of students, inappropriate interactions with students, or refusal to perform job duties as assigned. As you encounter a difficult situation, assess the seriousness and consequences as it relates to the work of the school. Then consider what needs to happen and your responsibility in those next steps.

▶ *As the School Administrator, How Do I Decide What Is within My Responsibility and Control, and What Is Completely Outside of My Circle of Control and I Need to Simply Let Go?*

There is no clear-cut answer to this question. At the same time, the quandary in your mind might be the result of self-imposed self-doubt and this is perhaps the most troubling internal dispute we have as school leaders. What should I do, if anything? Am I justified in acting? Is this a big deal or is it just irritating to me? As school leaders, we simply must continue to contemplate, is this mine to deal with, shall I continue to try to empower the person to make changes for themselves, or is this something of which I need to let go altogether. It gets easier and clearer as you continue to gain experience and work with competent, confident, and successful school leaders. Let them help you. Below are some guiding principles that you might consider to help you determine the answer to these questions.

Remember, most parents, employees, and colleagues in your institution are not going to go away. The most important and most influential way to work productively with all of them is to have the best relationship possible, because they will be there again tomorrow. That means to handle them with care and clarity. Do not give mixed messages, be direct and at the same time remember they are human beings with perspectives of their own. Never give up. As difficult as someone may be, be kind, treat people with dignity, listen, and think before you speak.

No matter who is talking to you, you can determine your boundaries. If someone is cursing at you or speaking in a way that is prohibiting the conversation from moving forward, discuss the expectations for a conversation and then end the meeting, if necessary. You do not have control over others; however, you have control over what you will and will not tolerate in your space or in the school environment.

When things happen, ask yourself this question, "What am I going to do about it?" Do not perseverate on the things you cannot control, rather consider if there is action for you to take. If there is no action to take, let it go. If it is impacting your school community and/or people within your school community, it is your responsibility to take action. Remember you have lots of control over yourself, so tap into that when it is appropriate. You may not be able to solve the actual problem today, but you can continue to talk with people who have the authority to do something about it and advocate for changes as you see fit.

Always have a trusted mentor with whom you can discuss your situations. Select carefully as these people may have significant influence over your decisions. Find people who you respect and admire, are successful and at peace, and who care about you as a friend or colleague. They should be a good listener, someone who will consider all sides and are not quick to diagnose or fix. They should also be knowledgeable about school administration. These are critical people in your leadership journey, whether you are in year 1 or year 30. Choose well and take care of those relationships!

▶ SUMMARY

Knowing your purpose, naming your past, understanding how others view you, taking care of you, and embracing your control are all components in the arena of self-awareness and working on you first. These are important because school leadership is hard, and if you are not okay, it is very difficult to focus on and take care of others, especially to the degree and fury that daily school administration demands. This chapter was meant to communicate the fact that it is widely believed, if you are confident, regulated, and thoughtful about who you are and why you are doing what you are doing, you are more likely to be able to approach leadership and difficult interactions more effectively.

REFLECTION EXERCISES

Overall

Consider how each part of this chapter is apparent in successful school leaders you know and how they apply these ideas to their own experiences. Does it make a difference in terms of how they handle different situations? Do you think their level of self-awareness preempts their success? How so? How does that correlate with their ability to have successful, difficult conversations?

Purpose

One exercise in determining your purpose is to make three columns, starting with your beliefs. Write down all the things you believe professionally and personally. You should write as much as you can think of, at least 10–20 belief statements. After you have written down your beliefs, list your regular behaviors in the second column. These would include actions or tasks you do currently, on a regular basis. Once you have listed as many beliefs and behaviors as you can think of, begin your third list in the third column, your strengths. What are you good at? What do you find interesting? What seems to come naturally to you?

Once you have your three columns filled, compare what you have written in all of them. How are they aligned? How are they not aligned? Are there links between the three lists? For example, do your beliefs have a correlation to your daily tasks? Are you able to have responsibility for things that are associated with what you value? Are you doing the things you are good at? Do your daily responsibilities include duties that you find interesting, fun, uncomplicated, or inspirational? If your lists are not compatible, why do you think that is? Step back and ask, does your current employment correlate to who you are and what you value?

Past

Make a display of the people you believe who have had the most influence in your growth and development. What is it about each of these people that influenced you the most? What character traits and dispositions do they carry with them? How do they present themselves? How do they connect with others? What is it about each person that entices you? What is now inherent in your attitudes, thinking, and behaviors, because of them?

Physical Wellness

1. Think about your physical health and why it is important to you.
2. Write down a few simple things you can incorporate that will make you feel better.
3. Set out some visual reminders.
4. Incorporate!
5. Document your progress, give yourself credit, and celebrate! Tell someone about it!

Emotional Wellness

1. Think about your emotional health and why it is important to you.
2. Write down a few simple things you can incorporate that will make you feel better.
3. Set out some visual reminders.
4. Incorporate!
5. Document your progress, give yourself credit, and celebrate! Tell someone about it!

Spiritual Wellness

1. Consider your beliefs and values. Where did they come from? How do you think they align with your reasons for choosing educational leadership? Do you think it has to do with something more powerful than a simple job choice? Why?
2. Write down a few simple things you can do that will help you think more about your reason for being. Contemplate your belief in something bigger than you.

Intellectual Wellness

1. Think about your intellectual health and why it is important to you.
2. Consider how interested you are in continuing to learn new things, engage with other people, and increase your knowledge.
3. Plan to learn new things every day. Reflect on your new learning.

Social Wellness

1. Do you feel motivated and energized by others or do you dread social interactions?
2. What value do you find in interactions with others at work?
3. How might all of this impact your leadership capacity?
4. Are there things you can do to enhance your interest in being around others?
5. Picture those people in your inner circle who you trust and rely on in challenging situations.
6. Is it worth thinking about spending more time with them? How might you do that?

Occupational Wellness

1. What is your purpose for educational leadership?
2. Why did you choose this path in the first place? Be sure to think about "why" you are doing it, not "what" you get out of it.
3. How is this position, in this district, fulfilling that purpose?
4. What kinds of things are you responsible for that have a direct link to your why?
5. What is most fulfilling to you in this position?
6. Is the time and effort you spend worth it, as you are pursuing your mission in work and life?

Control

List all the things you believe you control. Most of us will discover that we actually have enormous control, more than we allow ourselves to use. Discuss this concept with others whom you admire. After some thought, you might reconsider the vast limits of your own power.

Make a list of the things that seem to bother you the most, or keep you from engaging in meaningful rest or valuable time with those you love. Think seriously about each one. Is it something you can do anything about or is it completely outside your circle of control? How can you exercise your own control in this situation rather than let that person or thing control your thoughts and emotions? Practice letting go of things over which you have no power. Replace your thoughts with something you choose.

Bibliography

Bolman, L. G. & Deal, T. E. (2001). *Leading with Soul: An Uncommon Journey of Spirit*. Jossey-Bass.

Cloud, H. (2016). *The Power of the Other: The Startling Effect Other People Have on You, from the Boardroom to the Bedroom and Beyond – and What to Do About it*. Harper Collins.

Cobb, F. (2017). *Leading While Black: Reflections on the Racial Realities of Black School Leaders Through the Obama Era and Beyond*. Peter Lang Publishing Incorporated.

Corum, P. & Corum, B. (2023). *Missouri Leadership Development System (MLDS): Aspiring Level Participant Guide. Missouri Department of Elementary and Secondary Education,* https://dese.mo.gov/media/pdf/aspiring-level-participant-guide-4

Covey, S. R. (2004). *The 7 Habits of Highly Effective People*. Free Press.

Dungy, T. (2010). *The Mentor Leader: Secrets to Building People and Teams that Win Consistently*. Tyndale Momentum.

Harvard Business Review. (2021). *HBR's 10 Must Reads on Managing Yourself* (Vol. 2). Harvard Business Review Press.

National Wellness Institute. (2025). The Six Dimensions of Wellness. Wellness Alliance. https://nationalwellness.org/resources/six-dimensions-of-wellness/

Oxford University Press (n.d.). https://www.oed.com

Rath, T. (2008). *Strengths Based Leadership: Great Leaders, Teams, and Why People Follow*. Gallup Press.

Sinek, S. (2011). *Start with Why: How Great Leaders Inspire Everyone to Take Action*. Portfolio.

Prepare for the Conversation

Step 2

▶ THE IMPORTANCE OF PLANNING

We use this strategy all the time in life – preparation, planning, getting ready for something. We do it because we assume things will go better if we are prepared. We would never think to host a big dinner party for a houseful of guests without a plan. You might spend weeks in forethought, make trips to the store, and send messages to your guests. We know the value of planning. Whether it is an event, a vacation, or a simple night out, we give thought to the arrangements that must be made prior to an occasion. As educational leaders, we also plan. We plan faculty meetings, team meetings, academic time for students, and supervision schedules. Planning is a key part of our leadership responsibilities and there are many things we would not do without adequate preparation.

As a school administrator, you have many difficult or what could turn into difficult conversations. How much do you plan for those?

Preparing for these meetings can take some time, but is well worth it. Entering a controversial conversation ill-prepared can result in unpleasant and unexpected consequences.

Prior to having a difficult conversation with someone in your organization, it is important to have a general knowledge about where you

> Just as important as everything else we mentioned, maybe more, is the preparation for an important meeting, especially one that is between you and one other person, and one that could be contentious.

are. Start big and consider the context of your school and situation, looking at current policy, precedents, and the culture of the school. This is especially important for administrators who are new to a setting and may not know the history or the environment and its framework. Once you have a general understanding of your surroundings, the context, structure, and important rules, you can then prepare for a specific difficult conversation. This will include gathering information about the person with whom you are meeting, deciphering whether the concern is a pattern or a one-time event, being able to articulate the problem at hand, and knowing the purpose of the meeting. We will start with the broader context.

▶ KNOW POLICIES AND PRECEDENT

Many people with leadership tendencies have a vision, a desire to act, and a plan as you walk into a new position as an assistant principal, principal, or director in a school or district. You know what you believe. You know what you learned in graduate school and in your previous experiences, and you have already formed a vision of what this position will be like for you and others. You will probably begin to build relationships the way you always have, interact with others similarly to the way you did in your last position. This is what leaders inherently do. After all, you are an administrator, and you have the credentials to act, and the responsibility to perform. Just know, there might be some things to learn about where you are that will help guide you before you jump in with both feet.

Likely, as early as the first week on the job, there are important things to be done. You might need to complete the schedule, revise class lists, or approve spending. There may be individuals on staff who want your time and attention, have great ideas, or are wanting immediate considerations for certain things like changing room placement, altering their schedule, athletic considerations, or classroom materials. You are asked to make decisions even before you know much about the district or the school. Do you move forward? Do you make decisions based on your limited information?

We are all aware that every educational organization has formalized rules and expectations, usually in board policy, handbooks, or collective bargaining agreements. Even though we know these guidelines exist, it is tempting to move forward without considering those first. It is our leader-like instincts and our sense of urgency to make things happen. And too often, especially in the beginning, we simply do not consider what everyone else in the organization already understands. It is as if you went late to a party where people were playing games, and you began playing, even though the game had already started and you did not know the rules. You would probably not be very successful, or very well-liked by the other players.

> Almost every school administrator can tell you about a rookie mistake they made when they first entered a school because they were not aware of certain policies or procedures that were unique to that district.

School policies have usually taken years to develop and were not created by one person's idea or committee meeting. Rather, school boards and administrators spent months and years developing expectations for employees in the district. These mandates may have evolved after incidents that occurred in the district or neighboring districts, law changes, or years of contemplation about how a district envisions its community and educating children. That understanding can help as you move forward in your leadership of that community.

Board policy adopted by the Board of Education is not simply a suggestion. As a school district employee, it is your obligation to comply with policy. In fact, your contract probably says something about carrying out the duties as required by board policy. The expectations of the district through written policy are a cornerstone of your responsibility as a leader. As a school administrator it is also your job to hold others accountable to that policy. Every school leader should be keenly aware that in many situations you will encounter there are guidelines formally adopted and related to that issue. Those written rules require certain actions on your part and on the part of the employees under your charge. Your staff members are further away from the school board than you are, so your position as enforcer is fundamental to your job as school leader.

Along with policy, you should be aware of the relationship between the district and any workers association or union, (certified and classified staff) and what, if any, binding agreements are in place for those employee groups. This is where you often find things like parameters for after-school supervision, plan time, personal leave, calendar, and meeting requirements. You may also find within the association's agreement information about union representation in meetings, which will be important for you as you plan for difficult conversations with teachers and support staff.

A school leader must also know the expectation regarding observations and evaluations. What are the standards and expectations of the instructional staff? How are you required to document classroom observations? Is there a schedule of walk-throughs and observations you are required to follow? What about meetings after observations and feedback? Since one of the most critical jobs that a school administrator has is to support and grow teachers, and teaching quality is the most influential factor when it comes to student success, having a grasp on your district's expectations for instructional leadership is essential. As you gain an understanding of the district's policies, guidelines, agreements, and evaluation tools, begin to plan early as to how you will develop relationships with teachers and know their teaching. Share with teachers your plan to observe, support, and collaborate with them on effective instruction.

In addition to everything that is formally written down, you are going to want to know what is important to district leaders and your school community. These might be thought of as precedents that have been set, and not yet been memorialized in a formal policy. That might include holiday traditions, exchanging work hours from day to day, swapping duties with another employee, or dress code. It is good to have a clear picture of general district practices so that you can lead accordingly.

Finally, out of policy, precedent, and the people who are in the organization comes the school culture, that ambiguous and fuzzy concept that seems to say, "This is the way we do things around here," but it is not written down and can even be hard to articulate. The culture, or the feeling of the place, the behaviors and traditions, and what people find to be important within that school environment is critical to understand; however, you should not expect to understand it in the first few weeks. Pay attention, be aware, and observe people carefully. Know the culture existed long before you came and will exist long after you leave. Take the time to be still and watch, feel, and realize exactly what is important in that school. How do people feel and how do they treat each other? What is the tone and the mood? How will you acclimate to the culture, and as a leader, what will you do to influence it as you go?

▶ UNDERSTAND THE PERSON

If you are seasoned in the building, you will already know your environment. You will have likely dealt with other situations and you know what is expected of administrators and employees in your school district. For you, preparation for a specific difficult conversation will start here, with understanding the person with whom you are planning a difficult conversation. If you are new to a building as we discussed in the previous paragraphs, you could be doing two things at one time. Welcome to the world of administration. You will simultaneously be learning the organization, and at the same time, individuals in the school.

Whatever the case, the better you know the person and their situation, the smoother the conversation will go. How many times do employees get frustrated at an administrator for talking to them about something, and from the employee's perspective, the administrator has very little knowledge about the situation or the person in front of them? I remember teachers saying after classroom observations sometimes, "You have only been in my room a couple of times so you don't really know much about me or how I teach." This is a valid point. As supervisors whose responsibilities it is to evaluate other adults, it is critical that we have a clear picture of the person to whom we are providing feedback. That cannot happen in a few quick observations or in passing. We must watch, listen, ask questions, and really get to know the person if a fair assessment is going to follow.

A few important things related to really understanding the employee is knowing them as individuals as well as professionals. I am not suggesting we get too personal or invade a space where we are not wanted; however, knowing everything the person is willing to share with us, like interests, needs, goals, and strengths, is helpful. As a school leader make yourself available and listen. Show interest in people and who they are. Ask questions when you feel welcomed. Getting to know people is not only interesting, but also helpful as you work with them. Knowing people's attitudes, intentions, and actions will come in handy as you move forward with any potentially tough conversation.

Another thing to know about the person is their experience in education and how it has been perceived by them and by others. How do they describe their teaching and their success? What do past evaluations say? How do colleagues view them? A brief investigation about all of this will help you, not only connect with the person, but also understand where they are coming from when you may have to have a difficult conversation. If a teacher has had 25 years of good evaluations, is a strong teacher leader, and was named Teacher of the Year two years ago, it might not be a great idea to begin bombarding them with teaching strategies you feel they should be using. Remember, from their point of view, they are a successful teacher leader whose strategies have been affirmed year after year by the district, administrators, and colleagues. With this person, if there is something you think they need to change to be more effective, it would be in your best interest to get to know that person, understand their instructional strengths and leadership traits, and work with the teacher as a collaborator and thought partner. Allow them to share their knowledge and success with you. Learn from them. Understand them fully. Use them as a leader when new strategies in the field emerge. Invite them to weigh in and try them out. Make suggestions without putting down their work. Treat them as the leader they have been for years.

Maybe the situation is completely different from the one just described. Perhaps the teacher has taught for 25 years, displays anger and defensiveness, and has had problems in the past with other teachers. This could have been documented in past evaluations, which is good to know. When you observe their interactions, their teaching, and documents in their personnel file seek to find out more about the teacher. As you get to know the teacher through conversations, team meetings, and classroom observations, have informal conversations with them and understand everything you can about them. When you treat them with dignity and a genuine interest in their well-being, you will have a better chance of connecting with them and finding out what is really going on. If you are very successful, you will connect in a way that they are comfortable sharing their difficulties with you. Then, it will be time, if ever needed, to have a difficult conversation about expectations. When you know more first, you are likely to have a more successful and trusting connection, a better conversation, and more progress to follow.

▶ KNOW THEIR PATTERNS

Part of getting to know someone as a person is knowing their behavioral and attitudinal patterns. Let us say, for example, you enter a classroom and notice students are horsing around, no instruction is occurring, and the teacher is at their desk attending to something on the computer. Here is an important question. Is this a pattern or is it a one-time incident? Is this something that occurs all the time or is this something that is different from the normal classroom routine? Stay. Watch. See what happens. Then come back another day and observe again.

Watch them teach, watch students' reactions. Observe in the hallway, at passing time and before school. What do you see? How does the teacher generally interact with students? What typically happens during class? What is the environment like in the classroom? How are the relationships? Are lessons engaging? Is the teacher generally prepared? You can only know these things if you are in the classroom often, and if, while there, you are paying attention to everything.

> As you begin to give teachers feedback and have conversations with them about their teaching, it is important to know what occurs in their classrooms on a regular basis, not just once or twice during a semester.

In preparing for a conversation with a teacher, knowing their patterns is essential before you sit down with them, unless of course, you have observed something immoral, illegal, harmful, or severe. If you walk by a classroom and a teacher is berating and cursing at students, it must be dealt with immediately. In that case, due to the severity, whether or not it is a pattern is not important. What is important is for you to intervene instantly and deal with the current episode. In this case you would probably enter the classroom, use your walkie-talkie to ask for backup, approach the teacher with dignity, and ask if you can help. Encourage the teacher privately, without making a scene, to leave the classroom to calm down, supervise, and consult students until someone else enters to cover the classroom, and then meet with the teacher. Ultimately, in working with the teacher, you will need to know the full scope of the outburst and how common this is in their classroom, but right now, you are going to assess the situation you observed and deal with the issue at hand.

In another example, you notice one day after a test, students are allowed to sit for up to 30 minutes playing games on their devices, you might simply make a note. Then observe other times, other tests, other activities. If it is a pattern that there is a lack of student time on task, then it needs to be discussed. If it was something that occurred one time because the teacher realized at the last minute they needed to conference with individual students about their projects, then it is not a concern. It was simply the teacher's professional call based on what needed to happen that day with students. You will only know if you spend a considerable amount of time in classrooms, and if during that time, you are fully engaged in seeking an understanding of the teacher's patterns.

▶ ARTICULATE THE PROBLEM

We have been talking about preparing for a difficult conversation. First, consider your context, the policies and precedent, routines, and culture in your school and district. After that, we discussed understanding the person with whom you are considering a conversation. We discussed part of knowing the person is to know their patterns, what typically happens with them and their work, their students, their time, their attitudes, and so on. Knowing the context, the person, and their patterns should help you discover the next most important step, articulating the problem.

If you are considering having a difficult conversation with someone, there is likely a perceived problem. What is it? Can you articulate it clearly? Sometimes as school leaders, we know we need to have a conversation, but we have not yet fully articulated in our minds the exact nature of the concern. You may have a school custodian who appears to be disgruntled about work, who has been reported by others as being rude to other staff members, and who does not seem to be completing his responsibilities. You really know nothing further. Perhaps some of the concerns brought to you were by a person who seems to complain about a lot of different things, and the cleaning of the bathrooms is just one of many. So, is the incomplete work from only one person's perspective? Perhaps a lack of cleaning is happening lately because you are short one custodian. At this point, you do not fully know the problem, and therefore, it may not yet be time to meet. What is next, then? As the administrator, it is your job to get more information and learn what, if anything, is the problem. In this case, you might start with general informal meetings with all custodians, ask questions, and find out how everyone seems to be doing with their runs. This meeting could reveal good information not only from the custodian in question, but also from the entire team. It also allows them to weigh in and touch base about the fact that they are missing a custodian on their team.

If more information is still needed, be sure you are asking questions when people are reporting concerns to you. If someone says that a particular custodian is not cleaning the first-grade bathrooms fully, ask for specifics. What is not being cleaned? When do they notice it? How often? Have them show you the concern. Find out as much as you can. Sometimes, the observer is not fully aware of the entire situation. By showing you what they know, you can put those facts together with everything else and determine the scope of the problem.

Sometimes, as you are trying to determine the actual problem, it is necessary to talk with the person in question, not to deliver a message, but rather to seek more information. In this meeting, the purpose is to get to know the person, hear their assessments of their own performance and responsibilities, and let them know you are there to support them. This might be an integral step in determining if problems exist and if so, what the problems might be. In the custodial example, you may have gathered enough facts to determine that the floors in the first- and second-grade bathrooms are not being cleaned on a regular basis. You may have concluded it is probably not being done due to the school being short a custodian. Three people are trying to do the jobs that four normally do.

You also believe being short-staffed is the source of the alleged problem, and one of the custodians feels frustrated about the situation. After your preliminary work of collecting information, you decide to meet with the custodian to problem-solve next steps. In this case you now have a clear picture of the problem and can articulate the issue in the meeting. It might sound like this.

> Thank you for meeting with me today. As you know, I have been trying to get a full understanding of how everyone is working to make up for our lack of a second evening custodian. It seems like a lot of things are getting done between the three of you, and that is much appreciated. I know there is no way to get to everything. It seems like one thing we might be missing on a regular basis is the first and second grade restroom floors. Is that how you see it, and can you provide some insight to this? I'd like to brainstorm with you, and maybe we need to get the team together on this one.

▶ NAME THE PURPOSE FOR THE CONVERSATION

This brings us to identifying the purpose of the meeting. In other words, why are you going to meet with this person? Once you have a grip on your environment, who you are dealing with, and the alleged problem at hand, if you decide you need to have a conversation, you should craft the purpose of the meeting. Planning the purpose can give you a chance to articulate the reason for the conversation and what you hope to accomplish by the end of the meeting. You should consider if your purpose is too broad or not broad enough. Does it encompass what you are trying to accomplish for this meeting? Remember, Rome was not built in a day. You may realize there is going to be a lot to discuss with this person, yet in today's meeting you want to start with raising their awareness about a perceived issue and listen to how they view it. It may not be a realistic goal to also fix the problem in this meeting. That may be a follow-up conversation.

In the previous example with the custodian, once you have concluded the problems, the purpose of your next meeting could be to state the concern and get the custodian's opinion on it. It is a good idea to have one or two specific reasons for the meeting. Listing too many reasons all at once will cause the recipient to be overwhelmed and the crux of the message will be lost. If the alleged grumpy attitude is something that is not severe, let that ride for a while, and try to get to the bottom of the most significant issue at hand.

See how the first meeting goes once you state the concern about the restroom floors not being cleaned and ask for the custodian's insight and input. Perhaps in the next meeting, your purpose will be to relook at job duties, and what is being done and not being done because you are missing a custodian. You might choose to use your team to decide how you can rework the custodial runs so that the important things are being completed and everyone is sharing in the work. Eventually, if these meetings do not address the custodian feeling more positive and treating others better, you may also be meeting one-on-one with them to reiterate your support for getting job duties completed and remind them of your expectations about how we treat each other.

▶ PLAN FOR FOLLOW-UP

As you plan for the meeting, one last consideration is to spend time thinking about what kind of follow-up might be necessary. Interactions like these do not tend to happen in isolation. They happen in a series of meetings, dialogues, various forms of communication, or at least continued relationship building. When you are considering the problem and purpose of the conversation, you will want to give thought to what next steps will be necessary to continue the support and relationship. There are times in the preparation stage when you will not know what the follow-up will be because the purpose of this meeting is to hear the perspectives of the other person and assess next steps. If that is the case, no problem. Just be sure to plan that there will likely be some kind of follow-up. Without this in your preparation stage, you may forget this part, which can be one of the most important.

In the custodial example we have been discussing, the follow-up may look like regularly scheduled meetings with the custodial team to touch base, continue to support them, work with them as needs arise, and celebrate their hard work. It may be a follow-up meeting with the one custodian if that person continues to act rudely to others. In some cases, follow-up is casual and informal, because the problem was solved in the conversation. In other cases, the follow-up could be meticulous, explicit, and scheduled. In Step 5, we will explore seven reasons for follow-up and how to carry out conversations after the initial difficult meeting. They are listed here.

Follow Up to Touch Base
Follow Up to Show Support
Follow Up to Provide Feedback
Follow Up Because You Expect Action
Follow Up with Documentation
Follow Up to Correct Something You Did
Remember the Humans

▶ SUMMARY

Self-doubt is a powerful distractor for administrators as they consider having difficult conversations. In my training over the last several years, when asked what causes school leaders the most angst in having a difficult conversation, many of them say, "I spend a lot of time questioning myself and if this issue justifies me getting involved." We question ourselves as leaders because we do not want to put someone else in jeopardy if we are perhaps not seeing the situation clearly. We know there can be negative consequences of having a difficult conversation and we want to be very sure that our concerns are tangible and justified, before we enter that space. Ultimately, this lack of confidence causes many leaders to avoid the conversation altogether. Being well prepared for a difficult conversation can make all the difference in your level of certainty, your pursuit of the goal, and your success in the conversation.

There is a lot to do in preparation for a difficult conversation. In this chapter, we talked about the pre-meeting work and how you should arm yourself with the necessary information to determine that a discussion is necessary. These include knowing the policies and precedent in the district and school, understanding the person and their patterns, being able to articulate the problem clearly, and then determining the purpose for your meeting. Difficult conversations are hard to have, and the more you know and the more prepared you are, the better the conversation and the relationship to follow. Preparation helps you feel justified in approaching the situation, and it helps you define meaning so that your conversation has a distinct direction. With planning, your conversation is more focused and seems less massive. Once you have prepared, you can be ready to take one step at a time.

Your planning in this regard will not only help you with a better conversation, but it also shows the other person that you take the issue seriously, that you respect them and their time, and value their input on the situation. Great leaders take the time to plan for difficult conversations and the results are obvious. The meeting outcomes are more apparent, the relationship is protected as well as it can be, and the leader is confident and able to move on to the next step without emotional fallout.

REFLECTION EXERCISES

Consider a difficult conversation you know you need to have. How have you prepared? Considering this reading, are there other things you would like to consider prior to having the meeting?

What can you do to better plan for a conversation that will make it more focused, and the outcome more possible?

How beneficial is it to specifically name the problem before you meet? Why?

What part of preparation will you add to your routine?

Learn to Listen

▶ THE GIFT OF LISTENING

Think about what it feels like when you have something you want to share and the person you are sharing it with is fully engaged with you. They make eye contact, they stay with your story, and they ask questions about what you are saying so they can experience what you have experienced. They are not distracted by outside noises like phone vibrations or a passing siren. They stay with you. You can tell they are not thinking about something else or judging you, but rather they are listening to you, hearing your message, feeling your emotion, and wanting more. When true listening occurs, it is an enormous gift that is usually not forgotten.

> Listening is perhaps one of the most treasured gifts you can give to another person.

No doubt, you know many people who are talented at active listening. Hopefully you have friends, family members, and colleagues who are in that category. It might be the person you talk to when you have something serious to share or figure out. Usually, if you are in a crisis or have a problem you want to discuss, you go to someone who is going to listen to you, someone who will not divert the conversation, but rather focus on you and your situation at that time. Maybe it is someone who will give good advice, or perhaps they are best at asking good questions to allow you to think through your own circumstances. Consider how those conversations go and how you feel when they are over. What imprint does that person make on you when they engage with you so intently without hijacking the conversation or interrupting with a story of their own? We tend to gravitate toward good listeners when we have something important that we want to talk about. We find them calming, patient, and helpful as we work toward solutions.

Educational leaders who fully understand their community, can effectively solve problems, and have trusting relationships with others are, no doubt, good listeners. They understand others, connect through paying attention, and resolve issues because they seek to understand others before they make final decisions. Listening has many parts and enjoys countless benefits.

In this section, we will consider many aspects of actively listening as educational leaders.

> Administrators who take the time to understand listening, and practice good listening, will find more success than those leaders who want to do all the talking.

What does it mean to be a good listener? Abrahams and Groysberg (2021) describe it as having two purposes: one, to fully understand the messages and the emotions of the other person and two, to open the door for people to return to you with more information. If people do not feel fully listened to, they are less likely to share what they have to say. Effective school leaders describe good listening as totally comprehending the needs and perspectives of the other person.

Some people think of it as listening to remember so that as you continue to build a relationship with someone you can demonstrate you value them and remember what they have shared with you. Some describe good listening in terms of what it is not. It is not judging. It is not taking over the conversation to talk about you. It is not faking it. It is not thinking about your next comment. Effective listening might best be described as engaging in a level of listening that involves total immersion into the other person's thoughts. After all, we said what is listening, right? We did not say, what is it like to have a discussion about the best restaurants in your city? In this case, one person shares their favorite spot and then the other person shares theirs. In this chapter, we will focus on listening and we will spend a great amount of time on that and only that – listening.

Why spend an entire chapter on listening? Because it is truly a gift when you receive the real thing. Because as an educational leader, it will help you learn, connect, solve, discover, build trust, and lead. Because in a difficult conversation, it helps you understand the person and situation more thoroughly. Because people are not often used to having someone really listen to them. Because when it is done, listening has a multitude of positive effects for the sender and the receiver. Because listening is a gift.

In a difficult situation when there is a perceived problem, conflict, or high emotion, listening allows you to model calm, breathe, and understand the other person. In casual situations, it can be liberating to spend time with other people without worrying about what you are going to say. Instead, we hear about their last vacation. We ask questions about their latest redecorating endeavor. We learn about a new movie or book that just hit the market. Social situations can lead people to worry too much about themselves, their own words and messages, and what they have to share with others. It can actually be much more relaxing and entertaining to simply put others first, hear about them, and what they want to share. What does that have to do with leadership and difficult conversations? The transition is simple. When there is disagreement, or a contentious topic, start by listening. Understand where someone is coming from and why. Listen to their perspective and respect the fact that it may be different from yours. Listen fully without judgment, and try to fully comprehend. This gets you off the hot seat, releases you from the pressure of knowing what to say, and makes you smarter as you hear and understand someone else.

Listening also builds your credibility and the other person's trust in you. People often want their bosses to hear them out, consider their side, and understand their point of view. When they feel heard, your employees are more likely to share more and trust you. Consider again how it makes you feel when someone fully listens to you. As an administrator, when you give someone the gift of putting everything else aside, including your own judgment and perspectives, to listen to them, they will feel it! They will appreciate it and they will remember it. One of the greatest compliments a leader hears is when someone says, "You always listen to me." Employees know they will not always get what they want, and situations will not always go their way; however, if you have listened to, and understood their position, they will value that about you. Simply put, it will raise your credibility.

Another advantage of listening is that it makes you smarter. When you do all the talking, you are simply recycling everything that is already in your brain. You are repeating what you know, you are reiterating what you believe, and you are restating how you feel. You are not growing in your knowledge or understanding, you are simply reciting the same stuff that has been in your head for a while. When someone else adds to your information, and if you take the time to really understand what they are saying, you will actually learn something, perhaps another angle, more resources, other insights. If you truly listen to understand, you are wiser because you not only know how you think, but now you also know how someone else views a situation and why.

It is difficult to get everyone to collaborate and have ownership, if you are talking the entire time.

> In a difficult dilemma, like union negotiations, leadership meetings, or simple one-on-one problem-solving, you can facilitate the path to a better solution when you invite, accept, and value other perspectives. And then you must listen.

Maybe some people are wired to be better listeners than others. I am not sure about that; however, I do believe that we can all work on this skill. A person who is a good listener exhibits a demeanor that shows they value other people, and they care about what others have to say. People who listen without interrupting or talking about themselves throughout the conversation demonstrate a level of confidence and a disposition that is other-centered, as opposed to self-absorbed. They show others they are self-assured enough to be able to set aside their own needs and focus on what the other person is trying to say.

▶ PLAN FOR LISTENING

Great administrators not only listen well, they plan to listen. In their preparation for difficult conversations, they imagine themselves listening to the other person. They think of good questions that will elicit lots of information, they anticipate what it is they are hoping to learn. In their self-talk, they remind themselves of the importance of giving the other person space and time to talk. Active listening does not just happen for most of us. We may need to concentrate on what it is, its benefits, and how to effectively implement it. Here are some things to consider as you plan for listening.

▶ Put Away Distractions

As a school leader, there are emergencies that you must be available for, but most things are not emergencies, even though sometimes people think they are. If you are going into a 30-minute meeting with someone and do not want to be interrupted, most of us have an assistant to whom we can say, "Only get me if the building is on fire," which means I do not want to be interrupted unless it is a dire emergency. That also means the texts and messages that come in on your smart watch do not have to be looked at.

> While we have many devices that talk to us throughout the day, we must remember that we can control inanimate objects. You can put them away, you can turn them off, and you can choose not to look at them when they give an alert.

Every time you let a distraction take you away from the other person, you are sending a message that there are other things more important, including checking to see who just texted you.

▶ Think About the Other Person

Consider that they have perspectives, opinions, needs, and feelings. That does not mean they are not required to do the work asked of them, but if you want to get anywhere, listen to what they have to say. Perhaps they are requesting something very small from you that will help them get the job done better. Maybe there is a complete misunderstanding about what is expected. Maybe not, but you will never know unless you listen. Maybe you have already listened to this person for hours, and it is now time to give clear direction, document, and inform them of disciplinary action. Just remember that while different meetings have different purposes, be sure you have provided plenty of listening time when someone is struggling.

▶ Visualize Yourself as a Listener

Finally, one more way to plan for listening is to visualize yourself as a listener and practice it throughout the day. People who are good listeners do not just do it in a difficult conversation, or occasionally. They are good listeners all the time. That does not mean they never share about themselves, they do! And at the same time, they value what others have to say. Good leaders and effective listeners understand there is a balance in conversing with another person, and they can execute successful communication by listening first, and then sharing fittingly. Visualize good listening.

▶ MAKE LISTENING A HABIT

Making listening a habit happens over time, and if we think about it in every conversation, we can begin to make this part of our communication routine. One way to make listening a habit is to go through these steps in every conversation you have. Pretty soon, it will be natural and you will not have to give so much thought to making it happen. I call it "SHHH."

S – Shut up. Start with simply being quiet and letting the other person speak. Be silent. Let them finish. Look at them. Hear them out. Don't interrupt. When you think that they are finished, stay silent for a bit. There might be more coming!

H – Hear the message fully. Be sure you really understand what they are saying as fully as they want you to. For example, if a teacher says to you, "It was a rough morning in reading." Rather than saying, "I had a rough morning myself." Try saying, "Really, what happened?" Sounds simple, but often does not happen. Let them tell you!

H – Hover over what they said. Ask questions, or affirm their thoughts and feelings. For example,

TEACHER: It was a rough morning in reading.
YOU: Really, what happened?
TEACHER: I cannot seem to pull off the new reading curriculum. There are too many things to do at one time.
YOU: Which part were you trying to implement this morning?
TEACHER: Our objectives were to review blends with the new vocabulary and at the same time teach a new concept of prediction and also review characters and main idea.

YOU: That is a lot! How did you present it?

TEACHER: I told them everything we were going to learn today, practicing blends, making predictions, and naming the main idea and main characters. I think that was too much.

YOU: Did you think of a way to do it differently?

TEACHER: Yes, I'm only going to name one goal, like learning how to make predictions. The other stuff that is review, I'm just going to do it informally along the way. That way they will be more focused.

YOU: Sounds like you've got a plan. I think it's a good idea, especially with first graders to give one goal. That doesn't mean, like you said, that you cannot review other things, like having them highlight the blends in the story when they get back to their seats, but they know that in this lesson, you are mostly looking for them to predict the end of the story.

H – Have a good closure. This tells the other person that you heard them. It might include an invitation to talk more or simply a reassurance about what they said. In the current example, you could say, "Let me know if you want to talk more about this. I know this new curriculum is complex and we can certainly spend more time in our team meetings to share ideas if that would be helpful."

▶ LISTENING IN DIFFICULT SITUATIONS

How does this work in difficult conversations? It is a lifesaver, that's how! When we plan for purposeful listening, we are more likely to do it. When we visualize it, then we try harder to make it happen. Once the difficult conversation begins, start with listening. Channel your previous preparation and act as you practiced. Ask the good questions you prepared. Listen. Ask another one, and listen more. Remember when you are eliciting information from them, your focus is on them, not on you. If your purpose of the meeting is to also deliver a certain message or expectations, be prepared to do that as well, but remember, how you do that might be dependent on what they say, and how they say it. Consider this example, which is not necessarily one of the messiest conversations you will ever have, but as you prepare, you might begin to self-doubt since Steve is actually a pretty good teacher. He has positive relationships with students and some effective techniques. We sometimes avoid a conversation like this because it is not urgent. Watch how listening makes this conversation more collaborative.

STEVE THE STORYTELLER

You are preparing to meet with someone about a few observations you have made regarding students' lack of interest in class. The lessons are mostly lectures, and students sometimes seem bored, off task and uninterested. Your intent of the meeting is to find out how the teacher feels about the lack of student engagement. You are aware that the teacher has 11 years' experience and has all positive observations and evaluations in his file. He is a team player, supportive of other teachers, administration, and the district, and has good relationships with students. He spends a lot of time doing extracurricular activities with students. His name is Steve.

In your classroom observations, you have identified several of Steve's strengths, including interesting story-telling, relevance for students, and good alignment with school curriculum. The problem is, Steve gets very caught up in his stories, and forgets to involve the students. After a while, they lose interest and do not engage in the content as much as they could. Steve has so many strengths, and with a little bit of tweaking to engage students, you believe the energy in the room, student interest, and ultimately, student learning will be powerfully impacted.

Prior to this meeting, you have taken the opportunity to provide positive feedback to Steve for his positive engaging student interactions, and his command of the subject area. He knows that you have identified those as strengths and he seems to be comfortable with your feedback and conversations. This is a great opportunity for listening. The upcoming meeting regarding student engagement is a chance for you to listen, ask questions, and connect more!

Prior to meeting, it is important to think about what you want to know about Steve's perspectives on the situation. You might start with this outcome, and then follow up with some questions. "Steve, thanks for giving me some of your time today. You are an extremely valuable teacher and team member in our school. I appreciate your leadership in the building with other staff, especially our new teachers. We have talked about your strengths in teaching, and I want to reiterate the positive impact you have on your students. Today I want to talk to you about something very specific, something I think could have an impact on your students' learning. It is simply how much the students are engaged in the lessons.

As we have talked about, you introduce your topic beautifully with an interesting story that hooks the students right off the bat. The story has relevance to the lesson you are getting ready to teach. Your learners are really with you for the first ten minutes or so, and then, the longer the story, the more of them begin to disconnect. Let's think about this for a minute. What happens when they mentally check out? How does that impact your efforts to get them to learn a concept? How could their engagement, sooner, result in more of a connection to what you are teaching? Let me ask you some questions.

- Do you remember the time when, maybe after your creative introduction and story, you had students work together to develop their own ideas about the concept? I am thinking I saw this with a jigsaw you were doing once. Do you remember how you did that? What are some other times?
- Do you notice that when you give them opportunities to work in groups or pairs like that, there is more energy about the content?
- Do you ever notice that after the first few minutes of you talking to them, some of them become disengaged? What are some ways you could get them involved while you are lecturing and telling stories about the content?"

This conversation, while it is important and could have strong implications for Steve's effectiveness and student learning, probably will not be that difficult. You have already established rapport with Steve, and he is open to dialogue with you. In the scenario, you ask good questions and let Steve talk about it. You give him the space to reflect and develop his thinking. Then listen fully. Restate what he says to show you understand. Build on it. Assist Steve as he puts together ideas to engage students more. Further discussion with Steve will come from the way he talked about your suggestions for engaging students. Listening here is a great building block for his development. (We will discuss this scenario more in Step 4, Closure and Step 5, Follow-Up.)

Now let us consider another scenario, and perhaps a more challenging discussion where listening is important.

> ### **CONFIDENT CAROL**
>
> This is a teacher who is in her first year of teaching. It is early October. You have noticed that she is very outspoken about her self-perceived successes as well as her grievances about some of the more veteran teachers in the building. She is extremely confident in her ability to teach and connect with students; however, some of her behaviors are inappropriate. She uses very casual language with students, talks at length about her boyfriend and some of the social activities they do on the weekend, and has even put down other teachers for being "too old to teach" and "out of touch" in front of her students. Other teachers have described her as immature and have expressed concerns about her being on staff. Her name is Carol.
>
> Carol is not shy about her actions and attitudes. She believes she is just "being real" with students, and other teachers should behave more like her. In addition to her lack of professionalism and inappropriate interactions with students, she has shown that she has much to learn about teaching and learning. She views herself as very much the center of the classroom and most examples are about her, not about the students. She gives them some opportunities to engage with each other; however, the lessons are not well planned, there is often little structure, and as a result, students get off task easily. You have completed several informal classroom observations and walkthroughs and have noted all these things at different times.
>
> Up to this point, you have had a few casual conversations with Carol in passing, asking her questions about her lessons or what you observed. You also provided one formal observation very early in the school year; however, at that time, the lesson was not concerning, and students seemed mostly on task. Since then, you have noticed the troubling patterns of lack of professionalism, lack of thorough planning, and below-average classroom instruction. You have identified the problems clearly in your mind, and you are ready to meet formally about your concerns.

In this meeting, the purpose is two-fold – to thoroughly understand her thinking and to raise her awareness of your concerns. First, you plan to gain as much of an understanding about her and how she feels about her performance as possible. You are seeking her understanding of professional relationships, student interactions, and quality instruction. You want to know everything you can about her perspectives and knowledge. Second, you want to raise her awareness that how she talks about other teachers in the school and how she interacts with students, is not acceptable and will need to change. In addition, her lesson planning and implementation need improvement.

While you have messages to send, it will first be important to listen closely to her thoughts about her attitudes, behaviors, and teaching. How she responds to your questions is going to give you great insight into your plan for moving forward. This is a meeting that cannot wait, and it may take some time.

> I have been looking forward to our meeting today, Carol. You have been teaching a full two months now and I wanted the chance to hear how you think things are going. Teaching is not easy, and as a new teacher, there is so much to figure out. I have two goals for our meeting. First, I would like to hear your thoughts and perspectives on your teaching thus far, as well as how you are feeling about your relationships with staff and students. Second, I want to share some things that I have observed, and make you aware of certain expectations I have for you as we move forward. By the end of the hour, it is my goal that we have both had the opportunity to share, and that we are on the same page as you continue in your first year. Overall, I am here to support you and help you have a successful start. Does that sound ok?

I would stop here and listen. Let her respond. Let her react. Give her time to think. She may have questions. Be sure to allow space so that you can hear any initial reactions she has. Listen carefully. Listen to understand her thoughts, emotions, and intent. This will tell you a lot about her and her perspectives. Listening will help you determine how you might be working with Carol in the next few weeks and months. If she gets ahead of you, perhaps asking questions like, "Are you telling me you think I am not doing a good job?" You might simply respond with this. "As I said, I want to hear your thoughts and after that, I will share some of my observations and expectations."

Do not let Carol run the meeting! Stay on track and stick with your plan. What if she says, "I need to know if I am getting fired. I feel like I'm going to have a panic attack." You can assure her,

> Carol, you have only been teaching two months. Expect that you have a lot to learn, and that is what I am here for. Take a deep breath; you are not getting fired. I want to hear

from you. And then I'll share. And then we will talk about how I can best support you to have a great year.

Listening to her responses, like what just happened, gives you some good insight to her thinking. Be glad for that understanding, but do not let it derail your meeting.

Then proceed with questions. Upon asking each one, listen carefully for her message, tone, and emotion. Try to understand as fully as possible, not only her awareness of effectively teaching a good lesson, but also her opinion about professional behavior. Ultimately, you will determine the best way to develop her. Is she open and willing? Is she reluctant? Does she realize the implications of her behavior and how she talks to students and talks about other staff? Does she know there are things she does not know? During this meeting, resist the urge to make too many judgments before you hear her out. Give her space, time, silence, and assume good intent.

> Let's start by talking about your classroom instruction. As you know, I have been in several times, sometimes just a few minutes and sometimes longer. I'm wondering how you feel about your lessons in general. Are they going the way you had hoped? As you are learning the curriculum, and getting to know your students, how do you feel things are going?
>
> Are the lessons I observed this week and last week typical of what happens in your classroom? How so? Is there anything different that occurs, when I am there or not there?
>
> In those lessons you just talked about, how do you check during the lesson that students are understanding the concept? How else? Do you feel like you have a good handle on each student's progress as it relates to the goal? How do you know?
>
> What kinds of things are you working on as you are learning good instructional strategies?

It may be appropriate during the discussion to interject your observations about off-task behavior and students becoming disconnected, if you are still giving her a lot of time to share. Continue to be a great listener. You might intervene if she demonstrates a lack of understanding about planning or assessing student progress during the lesson, but you could always do that in the form of questions. Just be careful not to take over. Remember, this part of the meeting is to listen to her and completely know where she is coming from. The longer you can do that, the more you will understand. Follow-up questions might sound like this.

> I have noticed during math there is more off task behaviors as you are working with small groups at the table. I know you are aware because I saw you redirect those students. How are you dealing with that, and what changes are you trying to make so that students stay engaged when they are in their small groups? (Give her time to respond. Listen.)
>
> You just said that you are satisfied if half of your students understand the lesson. Let's talk about that. What about the other half of your class? What is your plan for them? Remember as their teacher, it is your responsibility to make sure all your students are learning, an expectation I have, and I share with the district and with the parents of your students.

Each bank of questions is going to center on different aspects, the first was instruction and now we will ask about professionalism.

> The second thing I would like to hear you talk about is how you feel you are doing with relationships. Relationships with the other teachers, for one is critical. Do you feel you are building good connections with them? How so?
>
> Carol, last week I heard you make a comment about a few of your colleagues and how 'outdated' they are. This was in front of some other teachers. Can you talk more about that?
>
> What does teacher professionalism mean to you, and how do think you are displaying it? Do you think it is important to show respect toward other adults, as a teacher and role model?
>
> What about relationships with your students? Talk about how you build those and what those interactions look like.
>
> How do you determine what is appropriate or not appropriate to talk with students about. For example, when I walked in yesterday, you were talking about what you and your boyfriend like to do on the weekends, which includes going to bars and staying out late. Tell me more about how you decide what to share with them personally?

Tell me why was that conversation a part of the lesson in math class with fifth graders?

While one purpose of this meeting is to listen and understand her, another is to raise her awareness of the concerns and why they are concerns. One way to do that is to ask specific, well-planned questions and let her talk. Likely, by the nature of the questions you ask, and by hearing herself talk, she is going to realize some of the concerns you have. So let that happen. Let her talk. Listen carefully.

The second purpose of this meeting is to make suggestions and share expectations. The best time to give direction on professional behavior or instructional expectations in cases like this one, may be immediately upon their disclosure. If she begins to get defensive or upset, it will be an opportunity for you to engage with her, hear her out, and open the door for more coaching and accountability.

Planning for listening and making listening habitual will help you as an educational leader in all scenarios, including the difficult ones. It even helps in personal and family settings, but we will save that for another book. **Listening gets you off the hot seat, it builds trust and credibility, it makes you smarter, and it paves the way for answers and solutions.** Listening, true listening, listening to understand and remember, listening for message, tone, emotion, and intent, and listening without judgment and without thinking about yourself are all lessons to be learned, practiced, and used on a regular basis.

REFLECTION EXERCISES

Next time someone is sharing with you, think about your listening. Are you grasping the entire message, the intent, and the emotion? If you had to repeat back everything the person shared tomorrow, would you be able to do that? Do they feel heard and listened to? How does it make you feel to completely immerse yourself in their story?

How do you think people would rate your listening? Would they say you care about them and their message or would they feel like you care more about sharing your own stories, interests, and needs?

Bibliography

Abrahams, R. & Groysberg, B. (December 21, 2021). How to Become a Better Listener. *Harvard Business Review.* https://hbr.org/2021/12/how-to-become-a-better-listener

Abrams, S. (2018). *Lead from the Outside: How to Build Your Future and Make Real Change.* Picador.

Autry, J. A. (2001). *The Servant Leader: How to Buil a Creative Team, Develop Great Morale, and Improve Bottom-Line Performance.* Three Rivers Press.

Brown, B. (2018). *Dare to Lead: Brave Work. Tough Conversations. Whole Hearts.* Random House.

Covey, S. R. (2004). *The 8th Habit: From Effectiveness to Greatness.* First Free Press.

Krzyzewski, M. (2000). *Leading with the Heart: Coach K's Successful Strategies for Basketball, Business, and Life.* Grand Central Publishing.

Ramsey, R. D. (2005). *What Matters Most for School Leaders: 25 Reminders of What Is Really Important.* Corwin Press.

Scott, K. (2019). *Radical Candor: Be a Kick-Ass Boss Without Losing Your Humanity.* St. Martin's Press.

Senge, P. M. (1990). *The Fifth Discipline: The Art & Practice of the Learning Organization.* Double Day.

Meet with Success

▶ IT IS TIME TO MEET

Now it is time to have the meeting for which you have prepared. This is when leaders tend to feel the most anxiety. Seek comfort in the fact that you have planned well, you know your purpose of the meeting, you are going to listen intently and allow for silence, and likely, it will go better than you think! In addition, give yourself some credit. You are human. It will not be perfect and that is ok. They are also human, and they probably want to connect and have this conversation go as well as possible, just like you do. You've got this!

A helpful tool is to consider chunking the conversation into different components as you go. This will help keep you on track and contribute to a successful outcome, hopefully the one you planned for. The following steps, name the outcome, ask good questions, use care and clarity, consider your delivery, and facilitate closure will help you and the other person work your way through the conversation with clarity, collaboration, and hopefully success.

▶ NAME THE OUTCOME

Knowing the intended outcome of a difficult conversation, or any conversation for that matter, can pay dividends in the end for you, for the listener, and for the possibility of a successful meeting. The concept of having an end in mind, has been repeated over and over by educators when we present lessons to students, write curriculum, construct new building projects, or implement new programs.

> No matter what we are getting ready to do, if we do not know where we are trying to go, how in the world will we get there?

The more clarity around the intended outcome, the more likely we are to arrive in the desired place. We can call it different things, like an objective or a goal. Whatever we call it, it simply means knowing what we are trying to accomplish by the end of the given time period. When preparing for a difficult conversation, one of the greatest strategies to ensure success is to name the outcome.

MARK THE MILD-MANNERED SPECIAL EDUCATION TEACHER

A colleague shared a story which illustrates the need for this preparation strategy beautifully. She is the Director of Special Education in a large school district and decided to meet with each first-year teacher in the spring of the school year. Her goal was to see how their year had gone, see if there was anything they wanted to talk about and ultimately, she wanted to show them support and gratitude for their work. It was meant to be informal in nature, and friendly. Because of the size of the district and the layers of administration, she had never sat down one-on-one with teachers like this for a casual conversation. She thought this would be a positive way to connect, as new teachers were thinking about getting ready for their second year in teaching.

At the time he was asked to come to the meeting, Mark, a first-year teacher, had not yet received a contract securing his position for the next school year. He had never met the director one-on-one. His impression of her was that she was business-like, busy, and important. He had no idea why they were meeting, only that she wanted to meet with him. As the director describes it, she invited him in and asked him to sit down. She remembers being excited about the meeting, even smiling as he walked in. She started with a series of questions, "How do you think things are going," "Is there anything you would do differently this year," "How have you been doing with compliance and paperwork?" On pins and needles, he cautiously answered the questions all the while, his mind racing. He wondered why he was there, what he had done wrong and if this was the meeting where he would be told that he would not be asked to return next year. He had heard horror stories from other beginning teachers in different school districts about meetings like this. He became so nervous and anxious; he could hardly think clearly about his answers. He kept playing scenarios in his mind, trying to recollect things he might have done that could have caused so much concern that it alerted the director. He must be in trouble, but he could not figure out why!

At the end of the long and uncomfortable (in Mark's mind) meeting, the director said, "Do you have any questions for me?" There was a period of silence and she noticed he looked troubled. She waited patiently for him to gather his thoughts. Silence filled the room. It was awkward. She was confused. Finally, Mark responded, "Am I getting fired?" It was meant to be such an easy, friendly meeting, but Mark did not know why he was there, and so he jumped to the worst possible assumption.

In our training, as my colleague was reminded of this strategy, Name the Outcome, she exclaimed, "Oh my, I could have handled my meeting with Mark so differently. All I would have had to do is this,"

> Thanks for coming here today, Mark. I am meeting with all our first-year teachers just to see how you are doing, how you feel your year went and to see if there is anything I can do to support you, as we move into year two. By the end of our conversation, I hope to know you better and have a clear understanding of how I might support our new teachers as you enter year two.

Simple. Just tell him why he is there. It could have saved him an hour's worth of grief. Had the director simply stated the outcome at the beginning, Mark would have been more comfortable and able to share openly his experiences.

Knowing and stating the outcome has several positive benefits. One, like in Mark's situation, it simply puts the other person at ease, knowing the reason for the meeting. In addition to that, and this one is significant for the leader, it can help you stay on track, knowing that you are not trying to solve all problems in one meeting. Consider Erica.

> ### ERICA THE EMPATHIC COORDINATOR
>
> You are preparing to meet with a curriculum coordinator, Erica who has publicly expressed concerns, on behalf of other teachers, about the new math curriculum, yet has not shared them with you. According to what you are hearing, Erica, who is typically very positive, has instead expressed some very serious attacks about the latest iteration of the math program, and how it will be taught. She is the curriculum coordinator, and as such, usually has a part in the selection of curriculum; however, this time she was on leave and did not get to take part. Erica also has teaching responsibilities and has always been a strong advocate and ear for other teachers.
>
> As the principal, and knowing Erica is an important teacher leader in the building, you want a trusting relationship where the two of you can discuss topics like this, and present collaborative support to other teachers. In this meeting, after your initial greetings, you might start with, "Thanks for meeting today, Erica. I think you have some concerns about the new curriculum and today, I would like to hear your honest thoughts. I am hoping, in this meeting, we can both share our thoughts and concerns honestly, and talk about what we might do to help ease the transition because I know teachers are feeling a lot of angst. I need your help. You have important information that is going to help me, and likely some good ideas for some solutions that will help everyone."

Maybe, because of who the person is (typically very positive), their patterns (very much a leader), the problem (this person is leading others to feel negatively) and the purpose (you are hoping to intervene, understand her concerns, and get her to work with you and not against you), you feel this is the best approach. Either way, by naming the reason for the meeting, both for you and for Erica, you can move forward much more smoothly. In this case, there are no hidden agendas, and no trickery. You are making it very clear that you want her to share her thinking, so that you can understand her perspectives and those of other teachers, and ultimately gain her cooperation in this matter.

Naming the outcome of the meeting is key. There may be a lot of moving parts; however, knowing exactly what you hope to accomplish in the meeting will help you plan. It will put the other person at ease, help you stay on track and hopefully will assist both of you in reaching a good resolution.

▶ ASK GOOD QUESTIONS

After being clear on your outcome for the meeting, it helps to construct a few thoughtful questions that will guide the meeting and allow the other person to talk.

Quite often, difficult conversations are about learning what is going on so that you can decide what messages need to be sent. The first meeting is more likely going to be an opportunity to learn rather than to tell.

Prior to a conversation, think about what you would like to know from the other person's perspective. What insights can they offer that will help get to a solution? Continuing with the scenario about Erica and the new math curriculum, effective questions might be something like this.

> If you have not thought about what you want to hear from the other person and how they might enlighten your understanding of the situation, then you might be tempted to talk too much.

- Tell me your thoughts about this curriculum and from your perspective, what is good about it, and what is problematic.
- As you talk to other teachers, is there anything else you think they are concerned about?
- Since this has already been adopted by the school board, meaning at this point, we are required to use it, have you thought of the most effective ways to do that in light of the concerns?
- How might we incorporate that?
- What can I do to help?
- Is there anything you need from me that could help you assist the teachers in being more positive about it, and using it effectively?

Obviously, questions will be tailored to the situation at hand, and taking time to prepare a few questions will help you stay on track and provide an opportunity for the other person to feel valued. You will find conversations about messy topics go much better when the other person has the space and permission to contribute to the conversation. Asking questions and listening to their viewpoint also goes a long way in building trust and credibility.

I always found it helpful to write down meaningful questions before going into a difficult conversation. It helped me stay on track in terms of the goal of the meeting, and reminded me of the things I wanted to hear the other person talk about. Often, conversations go in many directions and before you know it, you might find yourself talking about something completely different from the original intent of the meeting. Naming the outcome and preparing your relevant questions ahead of time, in writing will help!

▶ USE CARE AND CLARITY

It appears people have one of two tendencies when dealing with hard communication. Some people focus a lot on compassion and the relationship with the other person. Being kind helps people feel valued and shows them you care about them as a human being. People who have the tendency to be empathetic in their listening and show sensitivity in their messages, demonstrate they care very much about the relationship with the other person. They tend to be good shoulders to cry on. They are often seen as encouragers and good friends. Their roles are often that of counselors, social workers, grandparents, and coaches.

Other people, sometimes found in leadership roles, seem to care more about the clarity and straightforwardness of the message. These folks might be people who are good at getting things done. They have vision and goals; they know the tasks required and they are good at giving clear directions to others. They have nailed the skill of clarity, which is required of a good leader. Afterall, the point is to lead people to do things that are in the best interest of the organization. So, focusing on the lucidity of the message is critical. People who focus a lot on the message seem to like others who do the same. They are happy when communication is clear, tasks are accomplished and things can be crossed off the list!

So, what is the difference? Isn't it just a matter of different communication styles? Yes! And it seems like educational leaders are wired one way or the other. But that does not mean we cannot pay attention to this notion, and sprinkle a little care, or a little more clarity into our delivery, depending on which ingredient might be lacking.

First, let us look at care. To be effective in building relationships and meaningful connections, we should probably show we care about the other person, even when sending a difficult message. Effective leaders recognize the importance of building bridges and listening with all our senses to show compassion. We ask good questions that show we value their thinking. We are honest and transparent, and we choose our words with respect and dignity. We give people the gift of time, and complete attention.

You may be a person who does not typically think about this, and so it would be awkward to suddenly start asking someone about their family or feelings. At the same time, stop to recognize all that you may already do that shows you care, and be sure to continue to do those things.

> **NATE THE NICE GUY**
>
> A computer technician, Nate, in a school district training I was conducting, was contemplating this notion, and stated, "I don't think I'm good at this. I just want to fix the employee's computer so they can get back to work and I can get to the next person's issue." Interestingly, Nate was well known to the other employees in the training and to his comment, they replied, "Wait a second Nate. We feel like you are very good at this. You are patient with us, and when we have a problem, you always stay until we feel the issue is completely resolved." They went on, "You always treat us with respect, even though we know nothing about technology." One person replied, "When I need help and call the technology department, I feel so stupid, but I am always glad when you are the one to respond. You make me feel like I am not the only person who has ever had this kind of problem. You are very patient and kind."

While Nate is not asking to see pictures of the grandkids, or the wedding you attended over the weekend, he is kind and respectful. He does not act arrogant for the vast knowledge he has with technology, rather he patiently helps people who need help. It is important to understand that benevolence can take on different appearances, and simply treating people with respect, listening to their concern to the point that you can understand and fix the problem in a timely manner is certainly one way to show you care!

For leaders, especially those who tend to be more focused on clarity of the message rather than care, should also remember that showing compassion does not mean agreeing with everything the other person says. It means slowing down to focus on them and their message, thoughts, and emotions. It means understanding how you might help and support them. It means valuing them, their positions, and their words. It means assuming positive intent and engaging in a meaningful and respectful way.

If you are constantly focused on delivering the message without any regard for tone and how you treat the other person, stop, and think about that. Some administrators with whom I have worked, reflect about the way they send email messages for example. One stated in a training,

> I notice when I send an email, I start right in on the directive or the question I want to ask. I never say anything like, "I hope you are well," or "I hope you are having a good day." I just ask for what I need. While this is efficient, I have had people reply with statements that are clearly designed to get me to slow down. They might respond with, "Hi Jackie. Thanks for the email. I hope you are having a good day." Other people will do that with in-person communication. If you approach someone in the morning and immediately begin addressing a work situation, they might come back with, "Well, good morning to you too!" In other words, they are trying to tell you, "I am a human being, not just a worker. Please acknowledge that!"

Next is clarity of the message. Clarity is critical when you are a leader delivering information especially in difficult times. It means we state something with language that is understandable to the listener. It means we use direct language rather than passive or hidden messages. We think about what needs to be stated and we state it as concisely as possible. It is not mean, it is not patronizing, it is not humiliating. It is clear.

When a principal is talking to a staff member about the expectation that students be picked up from recess on time, a clear message may sound something like this.

> I have noticed the last several days you have shown up about 1:15 to pick up your students from recess. Recess is over at 1:10 and it is important to be on time so that the recess aide can get to his next duty.

That is very clear. It is not hateful or accusatory if in fact you have observed the behavior. Another example might be a situation where you have already spoken to an employee about turning in reports on time.

> Sherry, in the last several weeks, we have discussed twice the importance of me getting the attendance reports on time so the office staff can review them and submit them. You and I talked about your morning routines in the office, and how you will make this happen. This morning, once again, we did not receive them. What needs to happen so that you turn these in every morning by 7:00 a.m.? While some things are not that time sensitive, these are and as I explained before, there is no wiggle room. This time I will send you a reminder in writing and I expect you to turn these in on time from now on.

This is clear, but to make the messages even better, add compassion. In the first example, that sounds like this.

> I have been noticing the last few days that you have shown up about 1:15, instead of 1:10 to pick up your students from recess. That is unlike you! Is there something going on that I can help you with so that you can be there on time?

In that example, you have included one sentence that values them as a person with needs. At the same time, you have been very clear that they need to pick up their students at 1:10.

In the second example, you might add,

> I am happy to sit down again and help you figure out how to get this done each time. I know this is doable, and I know it is uncomfortable for you to have this conversation with me. How can I help?

Messages are not confusing and the statement contains dignity and respect. Leaders who pay attention to both care and clarity are better able to communicate difficult messages and maintain a relationship through adversity. They are confident in their ability to communicate.

> When clarity is coupled with care, the message is easier to accept, as one is allowed to maintain their dignity, and understand exactly what is being said to them.

▶ CONSIDER YOUR DELIVERY

At this point you have examined many steps to prepare for your difficult conversation. You have considered working on yourself first, the context in which you are working, planning for your meeting, and understanding the important act of good listening. You have contemplated naming the outcome for the meeting, preparing important and thoughtful questions, and using care and clarity in your message.

This section, Consider Your Delivery, presents 15 recommendations for school administrators when having a difficult conversation.

> Prepare to Invite, Name and Consider All Points of View
> Take a Break
> Silence is Golden
> Consider "Thank you" instead of "I'm sorry"
> Name your part in the Problem
> Do Not Talk about What You Do Not Know About
> Think About the Airspace
> Remember People's Level of Concern Varies: Respect That
> Consider Location and Time
> Consider Technology or No Technology
> Consider Alternatives to "However" and "But"
> In your Preparations, Think About Your Self-talk
> Treat People and the Situation with Dignity
> Avoid Binary Thinking
> Watch Your Intentional and Unintentional Messaging

Aside from everything that has already been stated, these considerations further develop your capacity to have a meaningful exchange in difficult terrain. It is recommended that readers reflect on each carefully, so these tools will be readily available when you execute a difficult conversation. These suggestions have proven successful over and over in difficult conversations held by principals, assistant principals, directors, and district leaders. They are communication strategies that can be utilized no matter what the conversation is about or with whom. Following the explanation of each consideration are recommendations for educational leaders.

▶ Prepare to Invite, Name, and Consider All Points of View

Think about the differences in eyewitness statements after an incident has occurred. They often vary greatly, because even when we watch the same thing, we see things through different lenses based on our own biases, experiences, memories, and cognitive schema. In a difficult conversation, it might be better not to spend too much time trying to evaluate the rightness or wrongness of a story. Instead, spend time understanding multiple perspectives and be sure you thoroughly understand each, and where it is coming from.

An example might be if two community members are arguing about trash in the town square. One person states, "The problem is, there are no trash cans for people to deposit their waste and so the trash ends up on the street." Someone else might respond, "I think the problem is the people around here. They are so disrespectful and they throw trash everywhere." Each perspective likely comes with a different set of beliefs and experiences. The important thing is, both can be true and should be considered, as individuals try to solve the problem. This problem might beg for more trash cans in addition to an appeal to the community to keep the town looking and feeling clean for its residents.

During a difficult conversation, write down (in list format, or randomly on a sheet of paper), all the things that seem to contribute to, or are a result of some issue, from various perspectives. When all stakeholders see the many issues in writing, they may begin to understand that there are different ways to look at a situation. We must consider all perspectives to effectively solve the problem. If two people are having a difficult conversation, each person will feel better knowing their viewpoint has been considered and valued the same as all the other viewpoints. People may be more willing to contribute to solutions when they believe their side has been heard.

▶ Educational Leadership

Consider this scenario. A teacher says to their principal, "These students are out of control every day after recess." The principal's thought might be, "This teacher does not implement good transition activities to help students get settled down after recess." Both can be true, so let us consider them both, and everything else that might be happening in this situation.

This class is always the last to be dismissed from recess because classes are dismissed in the order they get lined up and quiet. The conflict begins outside with the recess clerk yelling at the class, telling them they are never going to be the first to go because it takes them so long to get ready. Once they are dismissed to go into the building, there is no built-in transition time for students to calm down. They are directed to go immediately into math. In addition, these students walk the shortest distance from recess to the classroom, and therefore have not had much transition time to settle down. The students are in fifth grade, and like most other adolescents, full of social energy.

Use all that information to help move forward. Let the teacher know that you hear and understand their concern. Walk them through the entire scenario with all the facts from their perspective and yours.

> The students are out of control and hard to settle down.
> There is no built-in transition time.
> The end of recess is never smooth or positive for this class.
> Math might be a tough subject to enter right after recess.
> A good transition activity may be helpful.
> It might be good to elicit ideas from the students.
> This class seems to respond well to turning off the lights and listening to music.

This provides a basis for a good brainstorming session on solutions. It lets the teacher know, you value their thought, and it is worth considering along with all the other angles and insights.

▶ Take a Break

Sometimes conversations are *so* intense, we need a break, but we might not know how to facilitate that. When you determine it is time to "Take a Break," use this strategy, where you (figuratively) step out of the discussion, talk about any emotion or discomfort, and then, when it is time, come back. It might sound like this. "I notice we both seem to be feeling anxious right now," or "I'm not sure what happened, but I don't feel like we're getting anywhere with this" or, "Do you want to take a break for a few minutes, maybe get a drink, and come back?" This strategy is certainly not needed in all conversations, but it is a good one to have in your back pocket should things get stressful. The use of this strategy not only can relieve tension and help redirect the conversation, it also shows the person you care about them and their needs. Ultimately, this can have a positive impact on the discussion at hand as well as in future conversations.

▶ Educational Leadership

Emotions are often escalated when school administrators are speaking with individuals one-on-one in potentially contentious situations. This is an excellent technique to slow the process, demonstrate care, and work on building trust. It helps to facilitate more precision in our messages because emotions are dealt with first. School principals may find themselves using this strategy in meetings with parents of children who are experiencing extreme challenges in school. Meetings such as these can be an emotional quandary for a mom or a dad, and they are often overwhelmed by our position, sophisticated language, and the power we have as educators to make certain educational decisions for their children. It can be intimidating and frightening for a parent. Compassion, time, and consideration for those emotions are vital in conversations and relationships. This strategy should be coupled with good listening, silence, meaningful questions, transparency, and consideration for their perspectives.

Taking a break also proves helpful when dealing with employees who have demonstrated misconduct or their performance is not meeting expectations. These topics are extremely unpleasant, because people know the implications could be serious. Embarrassment, additional work on something, or ultimately loss of employment are all on the table. Learn not to plow through a conversation when the employee is emotional and unable to handle the message you are trying to convey. It is usually beneficial, with their permission, to stop, talk about questions the employee might have, emotional reactions at the time, or simply take a break, and then come back to the content. It builds trust and paves the way for a more productive exchange.

▶ Silence Is Golden

Let there be silence! There are lots of times to embrace silence in a difficult conversation. These can include:

After asking a question
When the other person begins to share and needs time to process
Right after you have shared a concern

Stop, be still, and allow time for the person to think and collect their thoughts. Stay focused and stay with them, without talking, without fidgeting, without looking at your phone! Simply embrace the silence with them. Welcome the time it takes for the other person to gather their courage to share with you. Resist the urge to fill that space with more of your own words. People admire those leaders who can be silent and allow time and space for quiet processing.

▶ Educational Leadership

Along with listening, embracing silence is a great lesson for people in general, especially leaders. So much can happen during silent moments. Your silence demonstrates maturity, confidence, and the patience to be still and wait. People sometimes need time to think, and leaders must provide that opportunity if we expect to have a meaningful conversation. If you want to simply state a problem, then state it. After you state it, it might be a good time to let that message sit with the person with whom you are meeting.

> Give them time to think in silence. Let your message linger without clouding the meaning with more words.

MATT THE MAINTENANCE MAN

Consider this conversation with Matt, a maintenance worker in your department. "Matt, we have had two conversations in the last two weeks about the expectation in this department to follow up all work orders with a completion tag. When I learned two weeks ago that you had not been doing it, we met to discuss it and you assured me you

> understood the process and would follow through. You did not. We met again last Wednesday, after no completion tags were done. You said you hated doing those, because you felt like it took too much time, time you could be spending on doing more work. That being said, you told me you understood it was required, and that there was a good reason to have that record of work. You said you would start doing them immediately. Four days have gone by, you worked all four of those days and I know accomplished several things, yet I see no completion tags in your queue." That might be a good place to stop and let there be silence. How will Matt respond? Give him time. The silence puts the responsibility for response on him. Let him think. If you have prepared well for this meeting, then you are prepared for what is next, an email follow-up perhaps, which you will provide, but first, the silence in this meeting can be very powerful.

Silence is also a good strategy when you are starting with little information and your intent is to gather more. Give the prompt to the person with whom you are meeting, and let there be silence so that they have time to construct their answer. In a situation like this, they should be doing most of the talking, not you.

TALIA THE TEXTER

> You have asked Talia, a first-year teacher to meet with you about an allegation that she has student numbers and is texting them individually, which violates your district's technology policy. "Talia, the reason I wanted to meet with you today is because it has been reported to me that you are texting with students individually on their personal cell phones from your personal cell phone. I believe you are aware of the policy on this, and I would like for you to tell me more about what is happening." Then be quiet. Depending on the situation and Talia's demeanor it may take her a while to respond, so stay still and be patient.

Silence, like listening, is such a powerful gift for educational leaders and perhaps should be utilized more. Not only does it give the other person time to think, you may find that it also helps you process, breathe, and consider different aspects of the circumstance.

▶ Consider "Thank You" Instead of "I'm Sorry"

At times we may find ourselves apologizing for something small. This might be done for a variety of reasons. Maybe we are trying to be kind by apologizing, even if we know we are not responsible for whatever happened. Maybe we want others to know we take responsibility for a large swath of the educational environment and will apologize anytime anything has occurred that should not have happened. Perhaps we are simply filling airspace in an awkward moment. Sometimes, it is not the best technique to say, "I'm sorry." It can give mixed or unintended messages to others. This does not mean it is never ok to apologize. Saying "I'm sorry" goes a long way in many situations and is welcomed when it is appropriate. However, sometimes, it is too much. Let us say you are bringing up a problem to someone and they blame you, stating that you should have known something was amiss and you did not do anything about it. If in that circumstance, you do not feel you have the responsibility to apologize, try, "Well, I appreciate you bringing it to my attention now. Thank you for doing that. Let's talk more about it."

▶ Educational Leadership

Saying "Thank you" instead of "I'm sorry" might be used when working with employees who seem to want to avoid taking any responsibility. Instead, they make it a habit to blame others, especially you. You want to value their opinions and you also want to let them know you are glad they brought it to your attention. At the same time, you realize that all their problems are not your responsibility, and it would be dangerous to affirm their accusations pointing to you every time they have a grievance.

You want to encourage them, while shifting the focus of blame to the focus of good communication and problem-solving. As a sidenote, many educational leaders, rather than saying "I'm sorry," will use, "I'm sorry you feel that way," which can also send mixed messages. Saying, "I'm sorry you feel that way," can feel patronizing to the other person in some cases, and may not always be the best approach. Instead, it might be better to simply replace the words "I'm sorry" with "Thank you!" It sounds like this. "Thanks for saying that. Let us talk about it," or, "Thank you for your patience with me getting back to you," or even, "You are good about bringing things to my attention, and reminding me if I forget. I appreciate that." Different situations call for different approaches, and this one can certainly come in handy.

▶ *Name Your Part in the Problem*

Naming your part of the problem may seem completely opposite of the other strategy we just discussed, consider "Thank you" instead of "I'm sorry." In this strategy, discussed by Susan Scott in Fierce Conversations (2002), Name Your Part in the Problem, rather than diverting alleged blame, you are taking responsibility for some part of the problem. Just like in the strategy above, this may not always be appropriate, but it can sometimes be the perfect approach. In this case, it is ok to say, "I am sorry." It may sound like,

> First I want to let you know I should have brought this to your attention earlier. You deserved to know it was on my mind and honestly, I was not sure how to bring it up. For waiting this long, I am sorry.

Taking responsibility for your legitimate part of the problem can help the other person feel at ease, and then, just might result in them agreeing to share their part of the problem.

▶ *Educational Leadership*

Sometimes leaders have a hard time saying, "I'm sorry" and the inability to say it, when you have had something to do with the problem, can get in the way of engaging honestly and fully with the other person. When leaders are authentic and transparent in their attempt to connect, and can admit when they have done something that was not helpful or might have caused harm, employees will have more respect for us as leaders, and may be more willing to follow. People want bosses who are down to earth and who do not see themselves as flawless. It is okay to show your vulnerability from time to time. We are human.

▶ Do Not Talk About What You Do Not Know About

It is that simple. If you are being blamed for something but there are missing facts, or if someone is asking how to do something and you lack details surrounding the situation, it is better to ask questions, try to learn more from their perspective, and then let them know you are going to need some time. Resist the urge to ramble, fill airspace, or respond, just to look like the leader. Clearly state that you need more information. Do not try to talk about something you do not know about. Give yourself time, let the other person know when you will get back to them and try to find answers. There is nothing worse for others, than hearing their principal talk about something, about which they know very little. Many people see through it and after a pattern of this behavior, you will likely lose trust and credibility. If you just start rambling, you could also give some very misguided information.

▶ Educational Leadership

Educational leaders can surely relate to this. We find ourselves needing to have expertise in not only educational curriculum, assessment, child development, building, grounds, and bus schedules, we also feel we have to be proficient in legal compliance, security details and specific medical matters, to name a few. Most of us do not have expertise in all fields. We are educators or experts in a particular area like food service, or transportation, not doctors and lawyers. It is always okay not to know something, if we are willing to find out. Helpful language to use might be, "I am not completely up to speed on what you are talking about. I would like to find out more and get back to you," or "Can you tell me more about what you know about this, and I will follow up."

A classic example of this can occur in teacher negotiations or in working with union representatives at the building level. People who represent others in an employee association may inherently take the side of the member or the association without a lot of understanding of the situation. In turn, you, the administrator may automatically take the side of the district without fully knowing what is happening. This is a great example of when you should NOT talk about the situation, rather ask good questions, and figure out what you need to know to move forward. Then, go do your homework! Consider this situation.

> ### UMA THE UNION PRESIDENT
>
> Uma, the union president, has asked to talk with the principal, Gene. Uma is concerned because in her words, "Several teachers are getting sick because of the mold in the west wing of the middle school." This is the first Gene has heard about this, and he is quite sure that the district maintenance director probably knows something about the alleged problem; however, he does not know anything for sure, so he starts by listening. Gene, a wise principal, after hearing her out says this. "Thank you for bringing this to my attention Uma. This is the first I have heard about it. Can you tell me more?" In his first conversation with Uma, he asked great questions which causes her to think about getting more information herself. "Tell me more about how you concluded there is mold back there. What exactly have the teachers told you about their illnesses? Can you tell me how many teachers have reported it? Do you know what the doctors have said so that we can investigate? Do you know if our maintenance department has tested for mold recently? I would like to have a list of the classrooms or hallways where mold is suspected so we can follow up if that has not already been done. Is there anything else I should know about this?"

It could have been Gene's first reaction to start talking about alleged mold in schools, how a lot of times, it is not mold when people think it is mold, and so on. It might be better to strategically select a few questions to ask, and then go find out more information. Your speech about people jumping to conclusions about mold, may come in handy once you have all the information. Or, you may learn that in fact, there is mold in your building. Withhold commentary until you find out more information.

▶ Think About the Airspace

Pretend for a minute that a small group of individuals is having a discussion, and each time someone speaks, a mist of a certain color fills the air. With each person, a different color is diffused and, in the end, the air is filled with different colors of mist, each showing how much airspace everyone filled with their comments. If there are four people, for example, maybe blue, green, yellow, and red, by the end of the conversation those four colors fill the airspace by the amount of time each person spoke. Maybe there is mostly green, a little blue, and not much yellow or red, each respective of their person's color, and based on how much they spoke.

By considering this visual, people might reflect on their own contributions to a conversation. Is it too much or too little? If you are the one taking up 80% of the airspace in what is meant to be a joint discussion, you might want to think about listening more, and speaking less. If your color is never dispersed, and you remain extremely quiet during the conversation, consider contributing more.

▶ Educational Leadership

This is a good strategy to teach teachers and staff. Educators seem to love to talk! Some monopolize committee or department meetings to the point that others are frustrated and decide to stay silent. When professionals have this visual in mind, they might be better equipped to allow others more time to talk. They can also be advised how to elicit responses from others, like "Ryan, we have not heard from you. Do you have any thoughts at this point?" Teachers can also teach their students this strategy; not a bad idea, but I recommend the adults master it first!

Another time this delivery consideration is helpful for school leaders is when you are planning for a meeting. If you are getting ready to investigate something, say an alleged harassment by one employee to another, you are first going to think of the questions you need to ask in your interviews. You should then plan that 80% or more of the airspace is going to be taken up by the person you are interviewing. It is not appropriate, nor do you have enough information yet to talk about the situation. Listen! Let them do the talking. Plan for the airspace to be taken up mostly by the other person, sharing what they know!

▶ Remember People's Level of Concern Varies: Respect That

Be prepared for this. Often, two individuals may enter a conversation with different levels of possible consequences. When your mother-in-law is sharing her expectations about holiday gatherings, she may simply be trying to include you in long-standing family traditions. If you are new to the family, you may feel intimidated and like she is dismissing your ideas, even though that may not be her intent. The mother-in-law would do well to consider the feelings of the new family member, even inviting her perspective into the conversation. While the mother-in-law may not think anything about it, her command in the family may be inherently overpowering, even though that is not her intent. She is the clear leader and matriarch. What she meant to be a simple, friendly conversation could come across more controlling to others, simply because of her status, longevity, and confident approach. Your level of anxiety is higher because you have "more to lose" in the family as a newcomer.

The same happens at work, or in community groups when the boss, or the main influencer speaks, there is inherent dominance, which can lead to others feeling very nervous. Right or wrong, it is simply a good thing to remember that the other person may have a different level of emotional investment in the conversation, and therefore we need to consider how we approach the conversation. There are different power structures in organizations, friendship groups, community teams, and even families. Levels of power can cause some to feel stress or pressure, even though that may not have been the intent.

▶ *Educational Leadership*

While as leaders we may engage in difficult conversations on a regular basis, many employees and constituents do not. Leaders should remember that every time a conversation which points out wrong-doing, poor performance, mere concerns, or anything even slightly gloom-ridden is most likely going to be an uncomfortable and rare event for many employees. Leaders should remember this every time they are having a difficult conversation, and proceed with care.

▶ **Consider Location and Time**

Where and when you meet is important, especially when you are wanting to have a serious conversation. Consider your location.

Will there be an audience? Is someone in close proximity who could observe and make judgments? Is the room private and comfortable? Is it "their turf" or "your turf" or have you selected a more neutral location? What messages are you sending by the place selected to have the meeting?

What about the time? Is this really a good time to have this conversation? How will that impact the person with whom you are meeting? If they are in the middle of something important, how will that impact the quality of your conversation and their willingness to fully engage? Is it necessary to give them a choice in the time, or is it important to meet at a certain time, based on the situation? It is worth taking a little time to consider the location and time of the meeting, especially if it is going to be messy or uncomfortable for one, or both parties.

▶ *Educational Leadership*

Given that schools have lots of people who can make and share observations, as well as make judgment, where and when we meet with individuals should be considered. When something should remain private and confidential, which is often the case for educational leaders dealing with personnel matters, we must put careful thought into the location and time of meetings held.

▶ **Consider Technology or No Technology**

As you put thought into the location and time of a meeting, also spend time considering which is better, to use technology to communicate the message, or to do it in person? We have so many devices and means to enhance our ability to connect with others, and no doubt, technology is quick and timely, and often extremely helpful. Technology is useful and can improve the message if you are wanting to send video, audio, or links to resources. This is why thinking about the purpose for the conversation is so important. What are you trying to accomplish, and how can it best be achieved?

In addition, we must consider how the message will be received by others, and it will be unhelpful or destructive if we choose to send a text, use a portal, or send an email. So often, messages are misinterpreted when they are written, because they inherently lack tone, body language, question, and answer. It is harder to show your desire to connect, and understand and solve a problem together. Even if someone starts the conversation on email, it might be best to respond in person or over the phone as opposed to responding via email. When messages are difficult, especially when they inherently solicit different perspectives and the need for discussion, it is almost always better to do it in person.

▶ *Educational Leadership*

TARA THE TEACHER OF THE YEAR

A school principal recalls a situation where she had completed a classroom observation with a teacher, Tara, and after being in the classroom for the entire lesson, she walked away with some concerns. Principal Pam had never sat down with this teacher, as she was a new administrator in the school. They had previously not communicated a lot, other than niceties in passing. This was the first formal observation and the first time Pam would be giving the teacher instructional feedback. She decided that rather than meeting with Tara, she would send the undesirable observation write-up to Tera's in email so that she could digest it before facing Pam. The principal quickly learned a lesson; this was a huge mistake for many reasons.

Tara has been in the building for longer than this new principal has been alive. She has a tremendous following of fellow teachers as a union representative, and has experienced 27 years of teaching, including favorable observations and evaluations by previous administrators. In addition, Tara was named the district's Teacher of the Year two years prior. You can imagine how she must have felt, getting this observation document in her inbox at 10:00 in the morning, in the middle of a typical day of teaching.

The teacher was filled with emotion, specifically anger and blame. She called a colleague and her husband during her lunch time, and began to plan her defense. She was not afraid because she knew she had tenure, a connection to the school board, and job security. She was more embarrassed and enraged that this "young, new administrator" would send something like this without talking to her about it first. She was irritated that Pam had not been in her classroom much during the year, and had not seen other lessons that in Tara's opinion, were exemplary. Rather, the principal chose this observation to use as the formal observation write-up. As she shared the news with other teachers, Pam was quickly losing credibility among her staff, a staff she barely knew.

Unfortunately, situations like this are not that unusual and happen when we are not paying attention to the consequences of our communication decisions. We will finish this scenario in Step 5, and show how Pam followed up after realizing her errors. But the point here is for administrators to consider their communication, when to use technology and when to have a conversation.

▶ Consider Alternatives to "However" and "But"

The use of the words however and but can invalidate the previous comment, which is often a positive. For example, if you say, "We have been good friends for a long time, **however ...**," anything you say after that may very well annul the first part of that sentence, at least in the mind of the receiver. Consider different ways to give messages so that all parts of the message stick. "We have been good friends for a long time **and because we have a close, working relationship and know each other so well**, I'm comfortable talking with you about this." This is a way to move the conversation forward, rather than reversing the positive statement you started with.

▶ Educational Leadership

So often, we want to start with something positive, so we do so and then follow it up with a "but" or "however." We must remember the impact this has on the listener. "You have had a great first year of teaching, and your students have been highly engaged in your lessons and are learning a lot." That is a powerful statement. If that statement is true and needs to be made, it should be made with a period at the end. The teacher should be able to process it. Maybe even follow it up with a question. "How do you feel as you think about your successes with students this year?" If something else needs to be discussed, like, "Today I want to talk with you about paperwork, specifically submitting grades on time," then do that.

You might not even choose to put them in the same conversation, rather have a different

> These two messages, high student engagement and submitting grades on time, are two different topics and two different feedback nuggets. Do not confuse one with the other, and whatever you do, do not put them in the same sentence!

meeting to talk about each. If you do put them together in the same conversation, at least separate them so the listener knows their strengths, has time to think about your positive feedback and reflect. Sit with it. Then if you want to also talk about an area of concern, make it known that there is something else you want to talk about. Be sure they can separate the two, and use their strengths to leverage improving on what needs to be better.

▶ In Your Preparations, Think About Your Self-Talk

We all talk to ourselves as we reflect on situations, and this self-talk can really impact how we come across to others. If in your mind, you are calling the other person a name or judging their work with sarcastic or rude language, that message may come across to them, even if you are not saying it out loud. Consider how you think about things and people. How do you narrate the story? If your thoughts include, "their work is bad," for example, you will want to just change the thinking to, "this work is out of compliance. I need to understand everything I can about the situation, make sure the teacher is clear on compliance mandates, and see how I can help them improve."

Let us say you are entering negotiations with the teacher association. Think about your frame of mind before you begin. Perhaps your circumstance is better served if your self-talk is,

> We are viewing this from two different perspectives. They have a certain role in the district and mine is incredibly different, causing us to see some of these issues very differently. At the same time, we have a lot in common. I am looking forward to understanding the needs of each other and coming to a common plan for positive resolution.

This will likely result in a better outcome than if you enter the space having already blamed or made judgment about the other person or the other side.

▶ Educational Leadership

As a leader, you are often the one who sets the tone for meetings, expectations for how we talk to each other, and frankly, habits

> We have the option to narrate our own story, so what will that be? Will it be an honest reflection about yourself and your responsibility, and optimistically seeking solutions or will it be blame, hopelessness and negativity? Your call!

within the school environment. Your frame of mind and self-talk is crucial. It guides the language you use and the actions you present. As a leader, it also guides the way others approach situations. This can be especially helpful when working with those people who are just starting to find their way. Many times, new teachers, and new leaders have not experienced certain things, like angry parents or disgruntled colleagues, and so they need help describing their situation.

▶ Treat People and the Situation with Dignity

We all face difficult people and situations which cause anger and frustration. We are human and it is natural to have those feelings rise up within yourself. Someone may not have earned your respect in your opinion, but they are human beings and can be recipients of dignified treatment. Treating people, and the situation with dignity means recognizing the seriousness of the situation, understanding the possible implications for the other person and the organization, taking the time to prepare, and then properly having a conversation with maturity and patience. We should consider our non-verbal communication, our comments, and the words we choose. A professional demeanor of decorum will pay dividends in the end.

▶ Educational Leadership

School administrators are often in the position of making judgments about people's performance and whether they will be promoted, transferred, disciplined, renewed, not renewed, or even terminated. This is a huge responsibility and should never be taken lightly. If a leader ever gets too comfortable with discipling or demoting individuals, it might be time to consider a different career path. That does not mean we do not do what needs to be done, it only means we must always consider the seriousness of the situation. We never fully know what someone is experiencing or has experienced in their past. We are not privy to all that has led up to this situation. And while those factors may or may not enter our decision-making process in this circumstance, we must remember that they are people too.

▶ Avoid Binary Thinking

This is a system of thinking that assumes there are only two possibilities, usually mutually exclusive. It often sounds like, either/or, or right/wrong. Be aware that binary thinking occurs, especially in difficult situations. When it does, it can make things even more difficult. One example might be, "Either we adopt this science curriculum, or I'm not teaching science." When our employees or parents come armed with this way of thinking, we must be prepared to help them think more broadly.

Binary thinking may be helpful sometimes. "We can go to the ballgame or we can go to the zoo, but we do not have time to do both." Unfortunately, it can also oversimplify situations, reducing your options and creativity. "Since the ballgame is today, we could do that now, and then go to the zoo over the weekend." By limiting the possibilities with "either/or," we might be overlooking certain nuances, clarity, and understandings that could lead to a better outcome.

▶ Educational Leadership

Sometimes leaders get caught up in the trap of others with accusations like, "If you don't suspend this student from my classroom, then you don't support me." This way of thinking can result in not only a difficult conversation but overall opposition and resentment about moving forward. In this case, using the aforementioned strategy, Invite, Name, and Understand all Points of View, can help to examine the situation more broadly. It is worth stating, "I do support you and I want to do that by investing time with you to discuss this situation and possible solutions." The bottom line is this.

> Let us not fall into the trap of either/or. I would like to think about the entire situation. What is happening with this student, why is it happening, how do you see the whole situation and what is happening from the student's perspective. I

would like you and me to brainstorm what supports can be put in place so that their needs are met, their behaviors are positive and you have what you need to help that student be successful.

▶ *Watch Your Intentional and Unintentional Messaging*

Intentional means done on purpose whereas, unintentional means not done on purpose. What kinds of messages do you send that are intentional and what messages might you be sending unintentionally? How we come across in a meeting, especially a difficult conversation, matters. It is worth reflecting on your verbal and non-verbal communication.

We should ruminate on this idea, prior to, during and after conversations. Think about your facial expressions, physical reactions, and how your non-verbal messages or even unintentional verbal statements may imply something other than what you were hoping. Reflect on your habits regularly, and during conversations, pay attention to what you are doing, how you are behaving, what messages you might be sending and how all of that may be perceived by the other person. Do you have a critical friend who provides professional feedback every now and then? If so, ask them if there are any non-verbal messages you are sending that you may not realize. You could also send surveys asking your stakeholders about your messaging. A recruiter who does almost all her work over the phone once recalled how she has a mirror on her desk to monitor her facial expressions while she is talking to, and listening to candidates. She believes, and rightly so, that if it comes across on her face, it likely comes across in her tone and through her messages, even across a telephone.

▶ *Educational Leadership*

School leaders are incredibly busy and they have dozens of issues on their minds at one time. Because of that, there is even more reason to think about your unintentional messages. While you might believe that you can listen to one teacher's problem while planning for an upcoming meeting in your head, while simultaneously monitoring students who are getting ready to misbehave at the lunch table, it is a pretty sure bet that the teacher expressing concern is not going to feel as if they are being heard. As leaders, we must think about what we are giving attention to at any given time. If you know a person needs you, and at this point you have other things going on, it is best to ask them if you can touch base with them later in the day, when you can give them your full attention, in a place that is private and quiet.

In a training once, while role-playing a difficult situation, a school leader noticed my eye contact throughout the scenario. He asked when it was over, "I noticed you maintained eye contact with the other person even when it got uncomfortable. You never looked away or leaned back. You physically remained very engaged." He wanted to know, "Did you do that on purpose, or was that just by chance?" The more you practice your communication habits, the more intentional you are with every move, and that was my answer. "I did it on purpose." We have to remember we are always sending messages, and the better we are at aligning those messages with our true intent, the more successful the communication.

▶ FACILITATE CLOSURE

Remember, when a supervisor is meeting with an employee, there is inherent anxiety and pressure. Due to the power structure and the possible implications (embarrassment, discipline, termination), the employee's mind can be in a lot of different places during difficult discussions. The leader may be saying one thing, but emotions and nerves may be so intense, the staff member is unable to listen and think clearly. Although the leader may be every bit as nervous as the employee, it is imperative that messages are clear and succinct.

A good follow-up to naming the outcome at the beginning of the meeting is to repeat it at the end of the meeting. There is nothing worse than leaving a meeting with uncertainty and confusion about what just occurred. When the outcome of the meeting is not clearly stated, this can happen. When there is no closure to the meeting, the outcome could have gotten lost. State what you are going to do in the beginning, and what you did in the end.

The closing should also include the next steps. This might be quick if the follow-up action is simple, or it might be more complex as in the following example. As we will discuss later, there will always be some kind of follow-up to a difficult conversation. You have planned for that and you will articulate it in the closing of your meeting, including what you are going to do next, what they are being expected to do next, and how you will come together again to discuss progress.

STEVE THE STORYTELLER (PART II)

At the end of your first meeting with Steve from Step 3, after good questions and active listening, you are going to give him an expectation which will set you up nicely for follow-up. "In light of our discussion, here is what I would like to suggest. I think it would be most helpful at the beginning of class, to let students know what they will be learning about, and specifically what you will be asking them to do in the next few minutes. You could tell them, for example, that today they are going to be able to make sensible predictions based on the text. Tell them you are going to start with a story about your dog. At the end of five minutes, you are going to stop and ask them to make several predictions based on the story you told, so they need to listen carefully. You shared in our last meeting; you think it would be helpful to set a timer. I believe you said you would set it for no more than seven minutes so that you are sure to stop yourself, and engage your students. Do you still think that sounds like a good plan?"

You will not give Steve too much to think about in the closing, but one final suggestion, that Steve seems to be able to handle is this. "Finally, I want you to think about how your lessons will engage every single student throughout the class period. You have talked about the success you had with gallery walks and with dry erase boards. If you cannot think of anything else, do those! In the meantime, be thinking about other ways to engage them, like writing a summary with a partner, using sticky notes to record main concepts and then categorizing them as a group, or illustrating concepts on paper and trading them for discussion. Whichever way you elect to do it, you will give input and information to your students for a certain amount of time, like 5–7 minutes, and then stop and have them deal directly with the content. That will make it more meaningful to them and they are more likely to learn it."

Be clear and make sure Steve knows how to do this. Repeat all three suggestions succinctly. "One, let students know what you are doing, and what you expect of them in a few minutes so that they are prepared to engage. Two, set a timer and stop after 5–7 minutes and let them do what you told them they would do. Three, repeat this throughout the lesson by engaging students throughout the entire class period." Then tell Steve how you will follow up with him. "In the next week or so I will come by your classroom to watch for student engagement. You and I will keep in close touch about what you are incorporating and how it seems to be working. How does that sound?"

Delivering this information in the closure makes the next steps very clear.

REFLECTION EXERCISES

Which of the 15 delivery considerations are your favorite, and which ones do you see yourself incorporating in difficult conversations? Think about writing these down somewhere so that you can refer, and pull them out when needed. Visualize what it would look like as you utilize different ones.

Prepare to Invite, Name and Consider All Points of View – Think about a situation when taking the time to consider everyone's viewpoint would be helpful. Why might it be beneficial to put it in writing in the middle of the table?

Take a Break – Think of a situation you have experienced, either as the administrator or the employee being talked to by an administrator. Would this have been helpful? Why or why not?

Silence is Golden – How good are you at letting there be silence? During what situations would the conversation benefit from more silence on your part?

Consider "Thank you" instead of "I'm sorry" – Think of a person or a time when this would have been helpful. How might you have tweaked your language to take the focus from blame, to effective communication?

Name Your Part of the Problem – Name a time when it would have been appropriate for you to name your part of the problem. How would you best say that?

Do Not Talk about What You Do Not Know About – Have you ever been caught up in a situation where you automatically started talking or answering the questions, even though you really did not know the circumstance in totality? How might you do that differently next time?

Think about Airspace – If you think about your own contributions to a discussion (or mist as in this example), where do you typically fall in terms of percentage of time spent talking? Are you conscientious about how much you talk compared to everyone else? Do you monopolize the conversation or not say enough? What could you do to make the conversation more equitable?

Remember People's Level of Concern Varies: Respect That – When is a time where it would be helpful for you to remember that others may have more anxiety during a conversation because of their stake in the situation?

Consider Location and Time – Do you put much thought to the location and time of a meeting? Why do you think it might be helpful in certain situations?

Consider Technology or No Technology – Have you ever emailed someone when you wished you would have met in person, or vice versa? What was the situation? How would it have gone differently if it was in person? How would you do it differently next time? Why?

Consider Alternatives to "However" and "But" – Is this language you use often ("however" or "but")? In what ways? What resonates with you as you read the previous paragraphs?

In Your Preparations, Think about Your Self-talk – How would you rate yourself on your self-talk? Does your narrative need to change? If so, why? How will you make that happen? How will that impact your conversations? How will it influence your feelings about yourself, and in turn your confidence as you enter difficult conversations?

Treat People and the situation with Dignity – In general, are you good at treating people with dignity, or is this something you would like to improve? Who is someone you respect in this regard? What are some behaviors and attitudes they employ as they work with others in difficult situations?

Avoid Binary Thinking – Have you ever been put in the trap of binary thinking? How did you get out of it? How might this consideration help in the future?

Watch your Intentional and Unintentional Messaging – Do you know if you are sending unintentional messages? How do you *know*? Is there something you want to change about that? Think of a colleague or personal friend who will be honest with you and ask for feedback.

Bibliography

Gordon, J. & Kelly, A. P. (2004). *Difficult Conversations Don't Have to Difficult: A Simple, Smart Way to Make Your Relationships and Team Better.* John Wiley & Sons, Inc.

Jones, J. & Vari, T. J. (2019). *Candid and Compassionate Feedback: Transforming Everyday Practice in Schools.* Routledge.

Maxwell, J. C. (2013). *How to Influence People: Make a Difference in Your World.* Thomas Nelson.

Scott, S. (2002). *Fierce Conversations: Achieving Success at Work & in Life, One Conversation at a Time.* Berkley.

Scroggins, C. (2017). *How to Lead When You're Not in Charge: Leveraging Influence When You Lack Authority.* Harper Collins.

Conversation Follow-Up

Step 5

Follow Up to Touch Base
Follow Up to Show Support
Follow Up to Provide Feedback
Follow Up Because You Expect Action
Follow Up with Documentation
Follow Up to Correct Something You Did
Remember the Humans

▶ WHY FOLLOW UP?

As you consider the steps in having a difficult conversation, it is important to also consider the follow-up.

Once a difficult conversation has been had, there is going to be some kind of follow-up. Effective follow-up after a difficult conversation will ultimately contribute to the overall outcome of the messy situation and the relationship thereafter.

> Most difficult conversations do not happen in isolation; rather, they are part of a series of conversations in attempts to support our staff, develop others, solve problems, or address concerns.

Follow-up takes on different forms because we do it for different reasons. Consider a hard conversation you have had with someone because of misconduct. The follow-up for this is going to be different from following up on a meeting where a beginning teacher is struggling, admitting deficiencies, and begging for help. Whatever the case, follow-up is important because it provides support to the other person, and continues to build the relationship. Having a tough conversation and then not following up can leave the other person feeling confused or uncertain about what to do next with the emotion experienced, the messages stated, or the directive given in the meeting.

One good time to think about follow-up is in the planning stage. As you prepare for a meeting, consider what might need to happen after the meeting takes place. This will help, as you share important information during the meeting, and allow the person to contemplate and plan for the next steps. Another time to think about specific follow-up is in the closing of the meeting. At this point, you will restate the intended outcome of the meeting, and together, assess your progress toward that goal. Then, you can clearly articulate what will happen next.

Different follow-up conversations and actions send different messages and have different objectives. Here are seven examples of why you might want to follow up.

Follow Up to Touch Base
Follow Up to Show Support
Follow Up to Provide Feedback
Follow Up Because You Expect Action
Follow Up with Documentation
Follow Up to Correct Something You Did
Remember the Humans

▶ FOLLOW UP TO TOUCH BASE

One thing a follow-up conversation can do is let the other person know you remember their needs, the conversation, and simply put, them. This connection further develops your credibility and helps to build trust with the other person. Whether the conversation happens to settle a disagreement, plant a seed about instructional improvement, or correct a wrong-doing, the relationship must continue and the other person should know that you are committed to whatever resolution was reached in the meeting. If it is simply to move on with a new understanding and appreciation for each other, do that. It may have been a conversation that you do not need to revisit; however, touching base with the other person and carrying on a collaborative partnership shows the person that you value them. Remember, people tend to want a connection with their leader, and if the last discussion you had with them was hard, or even a little uncomfortable, a friendly follow-up to simply show support will pay off as you go.

An example of following up to touch base might be this. An elementary music teacher is preparing for the fifth-grade spring musical, and informs students that if they would like to try out for any main part, they must stay after school. You receive a phone call from a parent who is upset by this, because it is almost impossible for her child to stay after school, due to the mom having two jobs and the child's transportation arrangements. He really wants to try out for a part in the musical. You decide to meet with the music teacher to share the concern, and ask her to allow students to try out during the school day, if they are unable to stay after school. The purpose of the meeting is to share your concern about the message this conveys to students who lack the flexibility to stay after due to parent work schedules, and to encourage her to change her practice in the interest of meeting all students' needs. You are aware that you will ultimately require her to expand the tryout schedule, but you would like for her to feel good about changing her protocol, and for her to come up with the decision herself.

During the meeting, she agrees to allow students to try out during the school day if needed, and seems to completely understand the reasoning and appreciates you bringing it to her attention. In this case, there is no real need to follow up, because you know that she is going to change the way she runs tryouts, and she even shares with you her message to parents. Therefore, your follow-up may simply be to check in and ask how tryouts are going. It might be interesting to know how many students elect to do it during the school day rather than after school, and perhaps how parents have responded to this change. You are simply showing her that you appreciate her efforts and understanding in meeting all student needs, and that you remain interested in the upcoming musical. This is an example of a follow-up to simply touch base.

▶ FOLLOW UP TO SHOW SUPPORT

Follow-up often takes the form of support, providing resources, and checking on people. This is part of building relationships, gaining trust, and making sure people feel valued and cared for as employees. Support can often look like informal conversations in the hallways about family, vacations, or personal interests. Having those exchanges with staff builds comradery, shows people you care, and demonstrates your realization they are more than an employee. Showing support often means you have interest in them as an aunt, a pet lover, or a runner for example.

Other times, specified support is called for. This can happen after a meeting where you both discovered resources or assistance is needed, perhaps from the district office. Often, school leaders will be the ones to provide help or direction for employees when it comes to leave, insurance, retirement questions, and so on. In these cases, it is critical that you not forget to follow up with the other person. You may not be providing all the information; however, if you promise to get back to someone with details, remember they are waiting for it. Consider Tyler.

TIMESHEET TYLER

A night custodian, Tyler has been leaving early due to some health concerns. Percy, the Principal, found out through another custodian who is having to complete all the cleaning when Tyler leaves. Percy also finds out that Tyler has not been clocking out early. If what the other custodian is saying is true, Tyler, an hourly employee is getting paid for time not worked. With this information, Percy is prepared to sit down with Tyler. The purpose of the conversation is to gather as much information as possible about his ability to stay at work, any concerns that are causing him not to be able to finish his shift, how he is documenting his time, and what assistance might be available in the district, if help is needed.

"Tyler, thanks for sitting down with me today. I understand there might be some things going on with you that are causing you to have to leave early on some occasions. The purpose of our meeting today is that I want to find out what is happening so I can figure out how to best help you under the circumstances. Can you tell me more about this situation?"

> Tyler becomes defensive and wants to know "who told" and "what is not being cleaned." As was stated in another scenario, those nuggets are not important right now; however, they are a real concern for Tyler as he sits in the principal's office. Percy responds, "The reason I am talking with you is because I want to know what is going on from you. I value you as an employee and if you need assistance right now, I want to know what that is, so I can help you and you can continue to work. We need to get to the bottom of what is going on, so we can explore together how we best move forward."

Tyler talks about his situation with Percy. He shares his current medical issues, and specifics about why he must leave. He tries to assure his boss that his work is getting done and the other night custodian has been good enough to step in and help. Percy continues to ask good questions and listen carefully before making any judgments. During this meeting, Percy wants to make sure that he explores every possibility about the situation and that he understands clearly.

"So, you said that about once or twice a week you need to leave early because you are feeling weak and like you are going to get sick. You indicated that you have doctors' appointments to do some tests and find out what is going on. Those will take place next week, and your daughter is taking you to those appointments. Now, tell me how you have been documenting your time." Tyler responds sheepishly. "Well, I just wrote down the normal time. I figured I worked harder in the time I was here, and when I get better, I can make up the time. I did not think it was a big deal." Percy wants to explore this further, but decides right now is not the time. "Ok, thank you for letting me know. We will revisit that later. In the meantime, write down all the days and times you left early. I am going to find out how to best handle that, and I will get back to you about that detail. I know you know, reporting time accurately is important, so from now on, be sure to put the exact time you left on your timesheet."

After finding out as much as he could, Percy ends this part of the conversation letting Tyler know that he is going to contact their benefits office to see what options he might have for taking time off, as well as human resources to find out how to deal with inaccurate time reported. Percy wants to be sure he has all the information before providing direction to Tyler. He also wants to focus mainly on his support for Tyler and how he is going to provide helpful information for him so that his job is not in danger.

Percy assures Tyler that he is going to find out how the district can support his needs, while following the rules at the same time. The meeting ended like this.

> Tyler, thank you for sharing all that with me today. I know it probably was not easy and I am sorry you are going through it. It sounds like your daughter is good help to you. To summarize, you are going to get more information from the doctors and try to take care of yourself and follow their orders. You will let me know as you get clarifying information that might impact your work schedule. You will also write down all the dates and times you left early and get that to me in the next day or two.
>
> I am going to contact our benefits office and human resources to find out what assistance we have in the district and how we should move forward to support you as you get the medical attention you need. I am aware you want to keep working as much as possible and I want to help facilitate that. We want you here as much as possible, and we also want you to take care of yourself. We are going to meet on Thursday at 3:00 when you arrive to discuss what we both find out. In the meantime, if you need to leave, be sure to let the other custodian know, and be sure to clock out, at the time you leave. I will ask the assistant principal to work with you both tomorrow on a modified schedule when this occurs, so that the most important things are getting cleaned. We are going to get through this, Tyler, and again, I so appreciate you sharing with me. I value you as an employee. Did I miss anything?

There are a few different things on which to follow up with Tyler. Making sure you continue your support and getting back to him is critical. It demonstrates that you will ensure he is complying with policies, like appropriately filling out his timesheet, and, you are going to help him with resources when it comes to his personal health. Perhaps most importantly, it shows Tyler, you value him, and it makes it easier for him to come share more information with you.

▶ FOLLOW UP TO PROVIDE FEEDBACK

Sometimes following up on a difficult conversation means being intentional about the feedback you provide. It is important not to let one conversation, or one problem that needs to be discussed, define the entire person or your relationship. Meaningful, instructional, and performance feedback is a critical responsibility in the life of an educational leader, and important to those people who work in the building. Continuing to give good feedback consistently and to everyone is a part of effective follow-up with professionals in the school.

Teachers, clerical staff, custodians, food service employees, and teacher assistants generally work very hard every day to help others. Teachers have spent hours planning lessons, grading papers, and considering different students and what they need to be more successful. When someone puts that much time and effort into a job that is all about serving others, it should not go unnoticed, especially by the school leaders. Unfortunately, too often it does. People like feedback. Conscientious employees want to talk about their craft with the people who are responsible for evaluating them. They want to share good things. They typically hope for a trusting relationship with their boss. They like to be noticed for what they do.

Building a community of feedback and conversation about our work can be energizing for our staff and it will contribute greatly to the school or department culture. As a school administrator, you do not have to go far to find evidence that employee satisfaction comes from being a part of a supportive team. Teachers and support staff want to be trusted to use the knowledge and skills they have to do their jobs. They want thought partners and bosses who work side-by-side. They want to be a part of a community where there is meaningful work. If they are strong educators, they seek a strong team and deep discussion about the science and art of teaching. If they feel that their administrators are only putting in their time managing minutia, or they are focused on goals that are self-serving, the best employees may simply find another place to work.

> ### STEVE THE STORYTELLER (PART III)
>
> In this episode, Steve, an 11-year teacher has good relationships with students, tells interesting stories, and has a great command of the curriculum. After several observations and informal feedback to the teacher about his strengths, you determine that there is one thing happening in Steve's classroom that seems to be hampering his students' engagement in learning. You have noticed that while his students enjoy him and have connected with him in the classroom and in extracurricular activities, during his lessons, his students lose interest after about the first ten minutes. They start out attentive; however, Steve's stories last longer than his students' attention span can handle. That, combined with his inherent style of lecturing as his main instructional strategy, students tend to mentally check out of the lesson, missing learning opportunities and key concepts.
>
> In Step 3, we outlined how you would begin the meeting with Steve, name the outcome, and let him know what you are observing. You have shared with him how you believe that students will be more interested in the content if they could engage throughout the lesson. While his stories are interesting, it is hard for learners to stay engrossed if they cannot do something with the information. In the first meeting, several questions were presented to Steve to guide his thinking about his engagement of students. In that meeting, your goal was that Steve would employ more interaction with students in his lessons. This was not simply a suggestion; rather, something you expect him to do. Otherwise, students are losing valuable learning time that cannot be recovered.
>
> In Step 4, we provided next steps for Steve, so the follow-up is concise and clear. Based on his initial responses and preferences about student engagement, you capitalize on his ideas and give specific next steps so he can incorporate some effective strategies which will take his students' learning to the next level.

Now, after having the discussion, brainstorming, giving clear expectations, here is what a follow-up conversation might look like. This demonstrates follow-up to provide feedback.

> Hi Steve. I want to touch base with you about our conversation last week regarding student engagement. We left the meeting with some specific ideas about how you could do that. I have had the opportunity three times to watch some of this happen in your classroom, and I saw some effective techniques. I cannot wait to tell you what I observed, but first, I want to hear you talk about it. Tell me

how you are feeling about your student engagement now that you are incorporating some new ideas.

Unfortunately, sometimes teachers like this one fly under the radar because as a principal you have far more immediate and problematic issues with which to deal. After all, Steve is not a bad teacher by any stretch. But think of the improvement you will make with him by giving him 20 or 30 minutes to brainstorm, not to mention the capacity to continually develop and grow. Since Steve is a teacher leader, he is an important person with whom you will want to gain trust and credibility. As a conscientious teacher, he will feel better when his teaching is more successful. He will also appreciate your time and partnership talking about good instruction. Even though this is an easy example, it is worth articulating. Too often, these are the conversations we avoid because we have bigger problems.

Meaningful conversations and productive feedback, should never end, because to support one another and stay on track, we should constantly talk about the good work that is happening, and the reason we are there. Like anything else, if a feedback system is in place, we are more likely to follow through and make it happen. When it becomes a habit, it tends to stay in place. An overall instructional goal can be that you initiate and maintain a schedule which provides regular and meaningful feedback, and conversations with all staff about teaching and learning, and their performance. It is a way to ensure that there is constant discussion in the school about the most important things happening, which are educating and supporting students. As you lead these efforts, you will inspire others to talk among themselves about their craft and the great things happening. You can build on what is good, and focus people's attention on teaching, learning, and service to others.

▶ FOLLOW UP BECAUSE YOU EXPECT ACTION

Another reason for follow-up is sometimes the topic at hand calls for action on the part of the employee. You will find that if someone perceives themselves to be "in trouble," they may not seek your assistance in the future. They may assume "no news is good news" and they will let the conversation drop if you do not follow up. In some cases, administrators feel they are working harder than the employee who needs to improve; however, this is sometimes the reality. If something needs to be fixed or improved, you must keep it on your to-do list, and make room in your calendar. As a school leader, this is your responsibility.

This kind of follow-up may be in the form of a professional improvement plan, or something less formal, like an email with steps to follow and an expected timeline. Make the expectations clear and then have a system in which you can observe and discuss progress with the employee. When you are following up with someone in this regard, it is important to be linear about your plan so that specific expectations are known, and how you will assess for completion has been discussed. This next episode is more structured than the example of Steve the Storyteller, because the teacher's attitudes and behaviors are more concerning and the timeline for intervention is more urgent.

CONFIDENT CAROL (PART II)

Carol is the very confident beginning teacher who has not yet demonstrated effective lesson planning or implementation. She is also struggling with appropriate relationships with other staff and boundaries with students. You met with her to hear her perspectives and learned she has little interest in changing. Imagine the meeting ended with her giving you a lot of reasons for why she teaches the way she does and how she approaches students and other staff. She is convinced that students will "eventually come around" and she does not believe in "pushing them too hard." She remains very confident in her convictions and seems to have little interest in changing the way she approaches lessons or people. She is firm in her belief about how she talks to and about other staff, and even her inappropriate conversations with students. She says things like, "This is just the way I am. If people do not like it, they are going to have to get over it."

You shared with her your general expectations and responses to her comments; however, she continues to dismiss your guidance as merely suggestions that she may or may not consider. At one point she says to you, "I know what you are suggesting may be the way teachers used to do things, but that's not the way we do it anymore." You ended your last meeting with this.

> Carol, our hour is almost up, so I want to draw this meeting to a close and let you know our next steps. Our purpose today was to get everything out on the table and discuss your thoughts and mine,

as well as expectations I have for you moving forward. I appreciate you being honest with me about your opinions and behaviors in teaching and in your professional relationships. It really helps me to understand where you are coming from and the work we need to do together.

First, let me summarize my expectations about your next steps on your lessons. Our goal is that all students are engaged during the entire lesson, every time. While I understand your desire to, as you said, "let them all come and go in and out of learning as they choose," this is not going to be the most effective way to help all students reach success. I am going to work with you on some strategies that I will expect you to implement as far as getting our learners interested and involved in the curriculum. Ultimately, it will result in better success for them. I will involve your mentor, Samantha, who has some great ideas and strategies that can help.

Second, I expect you to treat all the adults in this building with respect and courtesy. You need to refrain from making derogatory comments about people's ages or years of experience. You need to stop verbalizing your negative judgments about them to others, including your students. We have a staff ethics policy about how we treat each other around here, and we do not put down other staff the way you admitted you doing. Not only are you violating policy, this is no way to build trusting relationships with colleagues, who could be your biggest support in teaching. I will put that in writing to you as well as provide you with a copy of the policy I am referring to.

Finally, I would like for you to think about the conversations you have with students. You are their teacher and you have certain responsibility in terms of how you talk to them and what you share. I agree with you that it is important for students to be comfortable with you, and that getting to know a little bit about you is certainly okay. At the same time, we must be careful, knowing we are dealing with young children who are extremely impressionable. At this point, think about focusing more on getting to know them, their interests and learning needs and how you can help them grow and be successful at school. You need to be careful sharing specifics about your adult activities that you are involved in outside of school. You are working with fifth graders, so think about their level of maturity and what is most appropriate to share, in order to connect with them appropriately.

Carol, I believe you have a lot to offer as a teacher and I am going to help you. We will take one step at a time. I would like to meet again next week about your lesson plans. In the meantime, I am going to give you a couple of articles to read and templates we use for lesson planning. I think you will find this very helpful, and you will be happy with your student engagement and student learning as you make progress. I am excited to work with you. Do you have any questions about any of this?

This situation requires several forms of follow-up because action is expected, and by the way she responded, you are not exactly sure if or when she will comply. In all cases, you will weigh the severity of someone's comments and actions to determine how you will follow up. In this case, follow-up with Carol will include documentation of the meeting and her comments, ongoing meetings and likely, further written plans and progress reports. This is a good example of follow-up because you expect action, as well as the next section, follow up with documentation.

▶ FOLLOW UP WITH DOCUMENTATION

Sometimes follow-up takes the form of documentation. Any good human resources professional or school attorney will tell you, document, document, document. There are two ways to think about documentation as a school leader, formal and informal.

Informal documentation can be thought of as notes to yourself. These include your journal, your calendar, or your files, and are meant for your eyes only. They will help you stay on track, remember what you have done and what you are planning to do. Time is a funny thing. What can feel like two weeks, may have been two months and vice versa. Writing things down helps you remember the details of what happens and when. Refrain from depending on your own memory, especially where others are concerned. Make notes! Establish routines about WHERE you write certain things so that you can retrieve important information and dates as needed.

Formal documentation can take on a variety of methods, including an email to an employee summarizing a meeting, a disciplinary letter outlining expectations, a professional improvement plan, or an observation or evaluation form. I call this formal because it usually involves the employee having access to it, and can also be used in the future if needed. Think carefully about how you are formally documenting conversations and actions. Once something is presented to the employee and submitted into record, such as in email or the personnel file, it is difficult and sometimes impossible to take back. More so is the impact the write-up will have on the employee. This might be a good time to consult with a mentor about when it is appropriate to document and send.

For you, this is an important follow-up for which to plan. For the employee, and when necessary, this will ensure certain circumstances and expectations have been presented clearly and objectively, with the dates, policies, and other supporting evidence for the record. Here is an example where the documentation is formal, specific, and used for more follow-up.

MICHAEL THE MISTAKE MAKER

Michael is a first-year math teacher. In your first few observations in September, you notice that he seems to be struggling with the content he is teaching, specifically you noticed in two observations that he gave misinformation to students about basic formulas in math. He is teaching beginning algebra, so none of the students know that the information is incorrect; however, it causes confusion in their learning. You intervene and talk with Michael about it after your first observation, and he says he knows he errored in the one observation; he was just nervous because you were in the room. He tells you he corrected the misinformation with the students the next day. During the second observation, you notice something else that causes you to believe he is truly confused about some of the content. You meet with him again. He then admits that some of the curriculum is "over his head" and that he is studying every night to try to learn what he will be teaching the next day.

Obviously, this is serious. If a math teacher is lacking the content knowledge for the classes he teaches, swift intervention is necessary. While you may not have the subject expertise, you will need to take the lead in this situation. Why? Because if this comes down to dismissal, it will be your obligation, not that of someone else. This does not mean you cannot obtain assistance from an experienced algebra teacher with a great command of the subject matter, and the wisdom to be able to work confidentially with you and a new teacher. But you will guide the work. In this circumstance, urgency is needed!

Michael. Thank you for meeting with me today. We have had a few informal conversations about your presentation of some of the concepts you are teaching in basic algebra. You told me that you are studying at night to learn some of the material you are responsible for teaching, and have admitted to not being clear on all the concepts. I know you realize this; if students get the wrong information at the start, we might be setting them up for more confusion as they go. The purpose of our meeting today is to share information about your level of confidence in the subject matter, and how we can address the concern. We need to figure out what we are going to do about this right away.

I would allow Michael time to reflect on your comments. Give him the opportunity to speak openly, and share his thoughts and plans. This will help you make decisions about your next steps. He may say, for example, "You know, I have decided I am in way over my head and I was wondering if I could simply resign from my contract." In that case, work with your district leaders and human resources department on seriously considering taking him up on his offer. This very well could be the best solution in a situation like this. Students do not suffer, the district is released from paying him, and his salary can be used to pay and hire a replacement. It also allows Michael to find another job that suits him better.

It might not be that easy. Maybe Michael says, "Thank you for helping me. I need all the help I can get." Then, you know that he wants assistance and is going to try to improve. You must decide how much time you can give this, so as not to harm students. The good news is, he wants help. The quandary is getting him the level of support he needs, as soon as possible.

This scenario could also take another turn altogether. Instead of the first two examples, maybe Michael decides to fight. He might say something like,

> You are picking on me because I am an older first year teacher. Just because I made a few mistakes, I do not see what the big deal is. The kids are going to be fine. Just let me figure it out. I am calling my union representative. I have seen this before. You are discriminating against me because of my age.

Now you have a different issue. Again, you will need district support, and you have to make some decisions about the next steps. In this case, your work is cut out for you, because Michael does not see the concern, nor does he seem willing to work for improvement. You will likely and quickly, formalize an improvement plan which involves many observations and thorough documentation. In any of these three cases, the need for immediate attention is evident.

As a sidenote, this scenario proves why, in a situation like this, you would not "turn it over" to the department chair. You first need to determine the scope of the problem, the attitude and capacity of the teacher, and what your next steps will be. That is your job as the school administrator, and it should be discussed with your district leaders. Let us imagine in this case, Michael wants help. He is open to spending extra time after school with anyone who can assist him. He does not want to give students wrong information, and he understands his mistakes could be damaging for them in the long run. This is when you develop a formal plan with Michael, which will include action steps and timelines. You will hold him accountable. You will elicit help from an experienced math teacher in the building, and trust them to partner with you to support and improve Michael. And you will inform your district office administrators of your plan and receive guidance and support.

Your plan may be called a professional improvement plan in your district, or it may be less formal since you need to get something in place immediately. Because of the seriousness, it will be put in writing and you will implement it immediately. It is always a good idea to involve the teacher in the development of the plan; however, keep in mind, you will provide specific directives that need to be followed. You, or those who may be assisting you in the plan like the department chair or assistant principals, will then need to follow up every few days. It is imperative that students are getting correct instruction, so your classroom presence, or that of the math department chair will be critical. After your first few conversations and determining that Michael wants help, you meet to discuss your next steps.

> Thank you for sitting down with me today. As I stated in your meeting invitation, we will spend about an hour putting together a plan for you regarding the content you are struggling with and how to get on track. I have asked Sarah, the department chair, to join us for the last half of the meeting. When we finish today, we will have a succinct plan with clear action steps and a timeline so that you can get on track for your students. Do you have any questions?

Allow Michael time to talk and reflect. This may or may not be a difficult meeting for him, but be sure to answer his questions, and keep him on track. If, for example, he starts asking about his position for next year or if he is going to get fired, that is not a topic of conversation for today. Reiterate,

> That is not something I am prepared to discuss today, because we have some work to do first. Today and for the next few weeks we are going to focus on our plan. Let us concentrate on what you can do right now to get on track.

During your meeting with Michael, you will have developed an outline of the plan in terms of the actions that need to take place. These might include developing clear lesson plans that are turned in to you on a regular basis, reviewing the content with his mentor, and understanding that there will be constant observations of his lessons by the department chair, and by you. Michael can add details if he likes that might help him focus and succeed. During this meeting it will be important to stay on track, keep with the stated outcome of the meeting, and be direct about the fact that follow-up will occur.

In the upcoming weeks, as you work with Michael, share your observations with him and talk about how the progress is going. After the stated amount of time in the improvement plan, and once you have an adequate amount of documentation, you may discover that Michael is unable to effectively teach algebra at the level expected. You have worked with district office administrators to craft a plan for what to do next. Your meeting, after a month of observations and sharing progress data, might look like this.

> Michael, as I told you in the last email, the reason for this meeting is to discuss the progress of your improvement plan and let you know next steps. When we implemented this a month ago, I told you we would assist, observe, meet, and document for four weeks. We have done that and today I am going to summarize what I have, and then let you know what is next. Do you have any questions about our meeting today?

As always, give Michael the opportunity to respond, react or ask questions. The more prepared he is to hear the message, the better the conversation is likely to go. Often, people will accurately summarize the situation themselves, so give him that chance. Then take the time to review your documentation.

> I know this has not been easy and probably not the way you expected your first few two months in teaching to go. I owe it to you, though, to share the documentation so that you are clear. Since you have had access to this spreadsheet, I will try not to go into too much detail for which you are already aware, but I want you to feel free to stop me and ask questions at any time.

You will then proceed to share the documentation in an objective manner. Your messages should be straightforward without much commentary.

> "You were scheduled to meet with Sally for help sessions every Monday in October. On October 7 and October 21, you did not show up, and you texted her hours later in each case to let her know that you forgot. On October 9 and 17, I observed lessons where you were explaining polynomial equations, equations that have variables with positive exponents that cannot be negative numbers of fractions, however in some of your examples, you had negative exponents. A student called it to your attention, and you were unable to recover, telling the students you would have to get back to them. On October 23, Sally observed you assisting a confused student one-on-one and you were unable to help them with their questions. Sally stepped in to work with the student." You will continue to share each incident that is documented until you have summarized everything you have.
> "Michael, we have gone over a lot of information just now. Do you have any questions?"

Again, allow him the opportunity to speak. If he calls out one or two examples that he disagrees with some of the details, just listen. In this case, it is not necessary to go back and correct minutia, because it will not make a difference in the overall scenario or the outcome. You do not want to get caught up in details or his attempt to derail, which will not change the final assessment and subsequent outcome. Remember, you have prepared for this meeting with your district officials, and likely, the plan for next steps is not going to change, unless Michael brings significant news to the meeting. If you have been detailed in your reporting, and communicative with the department chair, that is likely not to occur. Do not allow Michael to derail the conversation. For example, here is what could happen.

> If Michael states, "I know you have all this in your spreadsheet, but I do not remember not showing up for those help sessions. I see where you have the texts where I told Sally I forgot, but I simply do not remember that. I think I was there. I am wondering if that has been falsified somehow." In this case, I would simply listen and then say, "This is the evidence I have of what happened. I trust that Sally has reported this accurately and that she has texts to support her documentation. Do you have any other questions?" Once you have supportive justification, like you do in this example, you should probably keep your responses brief. Allow him to respond and then move forward.
>
> His next comment might be, "I know Sally said those students were confused, but I do not think they were. Those kids are just not into algebra, and I think this is a bad example." Again, I would simply say, "Ok, is there anything else?" You are allowing him to respond, but your evidence is your evidence and if you are well prepared, there is no reason to go back and chase his bunny trails. When you have given him adequate opportunity to respond, proceed with the difficult message.
>
> "Michael, I believe you want what is best for students and I know this is not easy. Based on everything I have gone over, and with the coordination of our human resources department, here will be our next steps. You have a contract through the end of the school year. Your contract does not specify a placement, rather provides for employment in the district at a certain salary. What we are going to do is change your assignment to In-School Suspension (ISS)

teacher, beginning Monday. Your salary and hours will not change. The staff is aware that the position has been open, so I will let them know that you will be in that role for the remainder of the year. I will not be sharing any other details with them about your situation. You can tell them there was this opportunity and you have agreed to accept it. I expect that you will handle that professionally. On Friday, we will meet and talk about the routines for ISS, and what you will be expected to do. I will put all of this in writing for you and we will go over it on Friday. Do you have any questions?"

This scenario demonstrates the importance of documentation. Notice in the follow-up meetings, Michael wanted to argue some of the points. If you did not have good evidence with dates and specific details in writing, he might be more successful at defending his position and clouding the facts. Holding employees accountable is part of the job and unfortunately, not always an easy part. Sometimes, while this may be the most difficult follow-up, it can be the most important, and clear documentation here is key. Beginning administrators are usually not expected to handle these situations alone; however, it is imperative to understand your responsibility to spot situations like this and deal with them in the timely manner they deserve.

▶ FOLLOW UP TO CORRECT SOMETHING YOU DID

There will be times when you will regret something you said or presented to someone. Once you realize the negative implications of your actions, and how there might have been a better approach, remember, you have options. You can always return to the person and retract or restate the messages delivered. You can also prepare a message to restore any harm done and work on rebuilding trust.

Consider the conversation introduced in Step 4, Consider Technology or No Technology, where Principal Pam sent a negative observation write-up to Tara in an email. While there was not a "difficult conversation" that occurred, there was certainly a difficult situation and, in this case, Pam realized that she should have dealt with it entirely differently. Here is what she decides to do next.

TARA THE TEACHER OF THE YEAR (PART II)

Pam realizes she made a mistake by sending the observation via email. Not only that, she recognizes the lack of consideration she gave to Tara, an experienced and notably successful teacher leader in the school. With not much of a relationship to start with, no preceding positive feedback, no understanding of Tara and her tenure or her teaching, Pam sent negative feedback, over email with the hopes that Tara would read it, agree, and come down for a positive conversation. That did not occur. Pam realizes she needs to push the reset button. She decides not to make the same mistake twice, and rather than follow-up with email, she goes to Tara's room after school, a few days after the observation was delivered. She makes sure she is on Tara's turf, and no one else is around.

> Tara, first, I want to apologize to you. I made a rookie mistake; one I will never make again. During my classroom observation a few days ago, I observed a few things about your students' responses and I thought you would want to know. I subsequently made some suggestions for what I thought would be better instructional strategies. In trying to get my observation write-ups completed, I rushed to judgment, filled out the form and sent it to you via email. You are known to be a great teacher in this building, and I cannot imagine how my comments must have come across. I should spend more time in teachers' classrooms, including yours, before completing observation forms. It is my responsibility to understand you as a teacher, and not simply record a random classroom lesson as your formal observation. I should have known better. In addition, I should get to know you better and understand your teaching, prior to making judgments about strategies you may or may not have tried. Mostly, if I see something I want to talk to you about, I should come to you, ask questions, and discuss. You have certainly earned that respect, and I blew it. I apologize and now I hope, through this conversation and future ones, I can earn your trust so that we can work together collaboratively.

Tara stared blankly at Pam. She was not sure whether to believe her, call in a witness, get it in writing, or say thank you. She responded with,

> I appreciate you coming to talk to me, but it doesn't erase the fact that there is now a very negative observation in my file, a lot of which I disagree with because you don't know what lesson led up to this one and why we were doing what we were doing.

Pam let there be some silence to make sure Tara had shared everything she wanted to. Pam thought about how there really were some mishaps in the lesson, things that were not harmful to students, but could have been delivered better. But in the silence, as they were both contemplating these awkward moments, Pam knew that a few suggestions on teaching strategies will never be taken seriously by Tara, if this is the way she delivers it. The way to get someone like Tara to ponder her teaching is through collaboration, empowerment, and making sure Tara realizes that Pam is astute enough to value her as an experienced and effective teacher.

After some silence and space, Pam continues, "I have realized the importance of us building a relationship, and I need to understand more about what happens in your classroom. I do not ever want my observations of anyone to appear unfair or one-sided. That is not what fuels good teaching, collaboration, growth, or a strong school culture. I have not submitted the observation form into your personnel file and I am not going to. In fact, I have destroyed it. What I would rather do is sit down with you sometime, hear about your successes in your classroom, observe more, and build a connection so that we can talk openly about good strategies. I need to be more knowledgeable about teaching and learning in your classroom. I realize it will take some time for you to trust me and I understand that. I can only ask you to allow me to reboot."

Beyond that very difficult conversation, Pam has a lot to restore, but this is a good start. She is not backing down from anything. She simply realizes that she needs more information before she summarizes and presents a perceived negative observation. She also understands trust must be built for productive conversations to happen and solid relationships to be sustained. This is true especially when we are challenging experienced people to look at what they have done seamlessly for years.

Pam's follow-up will be ongoing. This conversation is a start. Next, she will visit the classroom, identify strengths, and let it be evident to Tara that she is interested in what is happening. When Pam sees something that she does not understand or that seems amiss, she will start by asking good questions and engage Tara in a collegially conversation. That will have to be done with patience and calm. Pam will understand that this follow-up will be a process and she will not necessarily be able to pivot in a brief period of time. Pam should be patient, not pushy, and continue to approach Tara in ways that respect her experience and expertise. She should not shy away from Tara simply because she made a mistake. She should also not revisit it. She apologized, told Tara she did not submit the observation summary and now it is time to move on.

▶ REMEMBER THE HUMANS

It is a good time to remember, we are dealing with human beings. As administrators it is easy to get so absorbed in your expectations of others, we forget we are dealing with people, not just problems. It is easy to be so immersed in the work, that we forget to remember the humanness of our employees. This does not mean abandon your expectations or your plan for feedback or improvement, it simply means people are living lives outside work. Treat them with dignity, value them as people, and interact with them regularly, in areas that are not part of a messy situation.

In this next example of follow-up, notice how the principal decides to focus on Rachel and their relationship, more than the behavior Rachel demonstrates, which is not bad or wrong, just not as productive as it could have been.

> Phil decides to concentrate on their connection and the problem at hand, and not the fact that Rachel went over his head to the superintendent about something. It results in them building a good relationship and even getting to know each other as people.

RACHEL THE REPORTER

Once a month, teacher representatives from the teacher union that represents teachers in the district, attend a meeting with the superintendent. It is called superintendent's advisory and teachers bring concerns they want the superintendent to know about in their schools. Sometimes the complaints are about their principals. Principals are not present at the meetings. This has been a long-standing tradition in this district, and teachers feel it gives them a vehicle to talk directly with the top administrator in charge.

Phil is a new principal in the district. His school's teacher representative and 25-year veteran in the district is Rachel who attends the meetings faithfully. It is still the beginning of the school year and up to this point Phil is unaware of the superintendent's advisory. He also lacks a thorough understanding of the teacher union's role in the district. One morning on Phil's way to work, the superintendent, Dr. Bert calls and asks Phil to stop by the district office. Unbeknownst to Phil, this is the morning after the first superintendent's advisory meeting of the year.

> Dr. Bert immediately starts the conversation upon Phil's entrance into his office, even before he has a chance to sit down. "We had our monthly advisory meeting last night with teachers, and Rachel attended from your building. She indicated that several teachers were upset because there are classrooms with broken and unusable shelving. She felt it was not only unsightly but unsafe. The teachers want something done about it." Dr. Bert is not particularly strong in the areas of making small talk, or showing compassion, before starting in on the message, but Phil is aware of that from previous conversations.
>
> Phil takes a seat and feels immense internal despair and embarrassment. First, he is in shock. He has no idea that the superintendent's advisory committee exists in that district. He is also surprised to hear about broken shelving because he has not noticed it, and no one at the school has brought it to his attention. He cannot believe that Rachel has not shared the concern with him. He thought they had a good working relationship. He is embarrassed, because as a new principal, he is expected to be able to take care of issues like this without them rising to the attention of the district superintendent. Now he wonders if Dr. Bert will ever trust him to run a school.
>
> Finally, Phil is angry because in his mind, people he trusts, Dr. Bert and Rachel did not give him the gift of clear, honest communication in a timely manner. He had no idea there was a monthly meeting called superintendent's advisory where Rachel would go and report grievances from his school. If Dr. Bert had shared this with Phil, he would have done some groundwork at his building prior to the first meeting. If Rachel had shared the concerns with him first, he could have done something about it, which would have solved the problem and never needed to be discussed in front of union representatives from all the schools in the district.

Phil finds himself feeling defensive. In this case, there was nothing he could have done to prepare himself, because he had no idea what was happening. Now, he is forced to respond. He knows enough to stay calm and not make this a big deal. He tries to channel his confidence and gratitude, and move forward. Fortunately, Phil knows just how to do this, although it takes him a minute to muster the courage. He embraces the bit of silence in the room to breathe and gain his composure, and when he is ready, he says the following.

> Well, Dr. Bert, thank you for letting me know. I am not aware of what Rachel is talking about but I will talk with her

as soon as I get to school and find out where the problems are. These will be taken care of immediately. Also, Dr. Bert, thank you for letting me know about the superintendent's advisory committee. I did not know about these meetings. I am glad that teachers have a voice directly to you and I am sure that they appreciate it. Finally, I am sorry that you had to spend time on this situation. I am going to try to open that line of communication better so that teachers will feel comfortable coming to me.

When Phil gets to school that morning, he finds Rachel in her classroom before students enter the building. "Good morning, Rachel. How are you this morning?" She responds with a friendly, "Hello" as she always does. "Hey, would you have a minute to talk about the broken shelves in our building? Dr. Bert said that there are several and I did not realize it."

Notice how Phil makes the broken shelves the center of the conversation, not the fact that she did not come to him first. This is important.

"Can you tell me more about where the broken shelves are and I am going to look at all of them today and work on getting them repaired immediately." Rachel responds, "Oh yes, here is the list of classrooms and the dates they were reported to me as broken." Rachel hands him the list, and Phil thanks her. "Oh, and just to be sure, has anyone reported any of these to the custodian, secretary, or an administrator? I do not remember hearing about this prior to this morning, and if we have a problem with people not responding to needs in the building, or if I failed to do something that was brought to my attention, I want to know about it." Rachel says, "Oh no, we just usually take things like this to the superintendent's advisory because we know they'll get done."

Now this is an important opportunity for Phil and one he capitalizes on right away. He is having a stress-free conversation with Rachel, and although he was feeling angry inside about an hour ago, he knows he has the chance now to build a bridge, if he handles himself appropriately.

> "Rachel, I really appreciate knowing this. I will take care of it immediately, and thank you for bringing it to someone's attention. I am hoping that in the future, you will feel comfortable bringing any concern to me, but until then, please continue to tell someone, so that I can address it. I do not know what it was like with your previous principal, but I want you to know that I take serious responsibility for this school and these kinds of things. If you tell me about them, I am going to deal with them." Rachel responds with a resounding, "Sure! That sounds great. It is just that our last principal never really cared about building issues, so we just took those to Dr. Bert and then they got fixed."

Phil has one more message for Rachel.

> "Oh, and I was thinking. I am wondering if it might be a good idea for you and me to meet once a week to go over things like this. It sounds like teachers are comfortable reporting things to you, so if you would be willing, I would like to hear the issues so that we can problem-solve and take care of things right away. Are you willing to do that?" Rachel was thrilled!

Rachel and Phil began meeting once a week to address concerns in the building. Most of the time, the meetings only lasted 10–15 minutes. The meetings were not just about building issues, they were also getting to know each other, learning about each other's families and personal interests. A solid relationship began to form. Problems in the building were discussed and addressed. And the impact spread. Rachel started telling other teachers that Phil was going to be a good principal, and that if they ever needed anything, he was willing to sit down and listen. Teachers began to feel more comfortable with him because of the testimony of their long-time teacher leader and friend, Rachel. All this started with how he reacted from one conversation after feeling shocked, embarrassed, and angry in the superintendent's office. It could have gone so much differently, but because of Phil's ability to think about Rachel as a human being first, they connected. Phil did not become defensive, he had confidence, understood what he could control, and what he could not control. He demonstrated a strong desire to connect positively and productively, one conversation at a time and with that, he built the foundation for a very important relationship with a teacher leader.

REFLECTION EXERCISES

How do you think following up after a difficult conversation contributes to building a positive relationship with the other person?

Are there times you can think of when a follow-up conversation might not have been necessary, but could have been a nice touch and put the other person at ease? What could that have looked like?

When following up because you expect action, how do you keep track of progress made or not made? Do you have an organized plan in place to ensure follow-up?

What did you think about Phil's response to Rachel the Reporter? Did you agree with his approach to focusing on building a communication bridge with her, rather than even mentioning the fact that she went over his head? Is there a situation you have where you might be better served by letting go of those things you cannot control (like her going to the superintendent), and focusing on the things you can (like setting up a better line of communication)?

Bibliography

Mayberry, M. (2024). *The Transformational Leader: How the World's Best Leaders Build Teams, Inspire Action, and Achieve Lasting Success.* John Wiley & Sons, Inc.

Keswin, R. (2019). *Bring Your Human to Work: 10 Surefire Ways to Design a Workplace that's Good for People, Great for Business, and Just Might Change the World.* McGraw Hill Education.

Final Remarks

▶ **CLOSING THOUGHTS**

Happiness, confidence, and the ability to connect successfully with others can improve when we reflect and learn effective strategies to approach people and situations with more focus and intention. The results of living a self-aware life, and utilizing certain communication strategies in conversations can turn the daily life of a school administrator from messy to meaningful. These considerations can also increase job satisfaction, make for better relationships, enhance your ability to problem-solve, and provide for a greater sense of balance and internal peace.

Educational leaders are faced regularly with difficult conversations for a variety of reasons, and depending on the nature of the circumstance, it usually requires patience, perspective, focus, and determination. The best school administrators can prepare themselves, plan for, carry out, and follow up on difficult conversations with success. To do that, we must be self-aware and confident. We must also be knowledgeable about our surroundings, the people with whom we work, the problems at hand, and the reasons to approach people and situations. After decades of educational leadership and watching hundreds of great leaders lead successfully, I began to practice all these attitudes and behaviors myself. I have attempted to share the best I know about building a strong you, connecting effectively with others, and communicating in a way that is caring, clear, and productive, even in the messiest situations.

Educational leadership is hard. In no time soon, will the overall structure of education, or the landscape of our positions change. At least for the near future, we will continue to be expected to perform many roles and serve a variety of people. State departments, school boards, district leaders, communities and school budgets will mandate we not only manage the day-to-day operations of a school or department, but also lead the efforts of effective instruction, inspire, and grow the adults who work in our schools, and make sure that our institutions are safe and meaningful places for students to learn and teachers to teach. As such, we have a responsibility to focus on our mission, vision, and values and try to stay on track for the sake of the people we are leading, and the children we are responsible for developing.

> Effective communication is a journey and we get better as we go.

Think about how much better you are at making a point, or listening to others, than you were many years ago. Leadership is also a journey of reflection. You will make mistakes, and you will learn from them and come out stronger. The better you know and accept yourself and others, the more you will increase your influence in a positive way. Life is also a journey, and we make many decisions along the way about how we choose to experience the expedition. I am honored that one decision you made was to read and consider the ideas in *How to Have a Difficult Conversation as an Educational Leader*. My wish is that you use, model, and teach others the ideas you found most intriguing, and you continue to reflect, so as you try to increase your impact on others in the world of education, you also find more peace and harmony in your life.

▶ CONSIDER YOUR NEXT DIFFICULT CONVERSATION

Carrying out a difficult conversation with success is not a checklist. It is generally not linear and it does not work the same every time, for every person. Hopefully, after considering the many aspects of preparing for, having, and following up on a difficult conversation, you have come to the conclusion that being a better communicator as an educational leader is multidimensional. At the same time, you are reflecting and working on self-awareness and becoming more confident, you are also practicing good listening with others. Simultaneous to thinking about using more clarity, or more care, depending on your tendencies, you are also considering the location of your meeting, the other person's possible reactions, and how to show them you value their perspectives by naming and inviting all points of view. In other words, you are stacking different strategies, behaviors, and dispositions, combining approach with attitude, and proceeding as if it is a journey, not a destination. That may sound too complex, but it is not. It just means, while there are strategies for success, you will have to try them, practice them, and use them in combination with other techniques to find what is most natural, most comfortable, and most successful for you.

As you prepare for your next difficult conversation, think about what you know about your context, the policies, and precedents set in the district where you are working. Consider the person with whom you are meeting and all that you know about them. Respect that and value them, even if they have made mistakes or the allegations are egregious. Know what is not in your control (their behaviors, their reactions, their emotions), and what is in your control (how you facilitate the meeting, keep it on track, respond to them, be clear, and move forward). Be sure your messages are not confusing, and do not be passive when it comes to stating next steps and expectations. Plan for follow-up. Listen. Embrace silence around awkward moments when it is their turn to talk. Remember the outcome of the meeting, state it over again in the meeting if needed. And end with it in your closing.

It is impossible to summarize the perfect way to have a difficult conversation, because every interaction between two people is different. Even the same two people will have different conversations depending on the day, topic, consequences, emotions, mood, and so on. The goal is that you have enough forethought, poise, and self-reliance that you can move forward with confidence and success every time. Keep all strategies in your back pocket and use them as needed. Know how to push the pause button when things get very tough, as in asking good questions and listening, or taking a break. Be true to yourself and be ready.

The only way to make it more natural and less stressful for you and the person with whom you are meeting, is to be more reflective yourself, and to practice effective communication on a regular basis. Prior to your next difficult conversation, practice some of the strategies you might want to use with someone else in an easier, less consequential gathering. This could be practicing self-talk prior to going out with a group of friends, using "thank you" instead of "I'm sorry" with a family member who seems to constantly blame you for something, or monitoring the airspace at dinner with your significant other. The more you use different strategies, and practice demonstrating the attitudes and confidence you wish to bring the table, the more natural it becomes and the more likely you are to be successful.

▶ MY HOPE FOR YOU

Thank you for reading this book. It is an honor to spend time with other educators and people who care about meaningful connections with others. From one educational leader to another, here is my hope for you.

As you start every morning after you awake, and before you rise, remind yourself about who you are, why you are, and what you are doing here. Review your mission as a human, and your vision for life. Spend time in your own spiritual enlightenment, thinking about what you believe. Then, get out of bed with a clear reason for starting the day. No matter what, this is your day.

As you go, never lose sight of the important lesson of taking care of you, and celebrate your daily habits that are positively and deliberately healthy. Remember, these are your choices. It is your body, your mind, and your soul. Take care of you, all of you.

As you engage with others, present with patience, perspective, and positive intent. Approach them with confidence and kindness. Own your attitude. Recognize your bravery.

As you communicate, do so with care and compassion. Listen with curiosity. Value others and their messages. Share your time, your attention, your interest. That is your gift to them. They appreciate you for that.

As you speak, have clarity in your messages. Believe that others can handle direct communication and clear dialogue. Enter the space with positive presupposition. Believe and remember, the other person is giving you the best they have at this time.

On this day, recognize your life is your journey. Your leadership success is your journey. Your ability to effectively communicate and deal with tough situations is also your journey. Embrace your growth, and your setbacks. You are human.

Remember to utilize all the control you have. Do not relinquish valuable time to those things over which you have no power. Take charge of your attitudes and your actions. Own your headspace, and do not let anyone in, without your permission. Protect your mind and your heart.

When your day comes to a close, know you have given the best you have. And tomorrow, if it is meant to be, you will have another day to share with others, work hard toward your vision, be satisfied, feel grateful, help people, and experience peace and harmony. For it is your journey, and not anyone else's. Embrace the time you have, and make it the best you've got.

For Product Safety Concerns and Information please contact our EU
representative GPSR@taylorandfrancis.com
Taylor & Francis Verlag GmbH, Kaufingerstraße 24, 80331 München, Germany